OH DEAR!
WHAT CAN THE MATTER BE?

MEMOIRS OF A PHYSICIAN
AND BUREAUCRAT

BY

RICHARD SHORT

TRAFFORD PUBLISHING

VICTORIA, B.C., CANADA

Canadian Cataloguing in Publication Data

Short, Richard, 1922-
  Oh dear! what can the matter be?

  ISBN 1-55212-452-5

  1. Short, Richard, 1922- 2. Physicians--Canada--Biography. 3.
Health services administrators--Canada. I. Title.
R464.S53A3 2000   610'.92   C00-911033-X

TRAFFORD

This book was published *on-demand* **in cooperation with Trafford Publishing.**
On-demand publishing is a unique process and service of making a book available for retail
sale to the public taking advantage of on-demand manufacturing and Internet marketing.
On-demand publishing includes promotions, retail sales, manufacturing, order fulfilment,
accounting and collecting royalties on behalf of the author.

Suite 6E, 2333 Government St., Victoria, B.C. V8T 4P4, CANADA
Phone   250-383-6864   Toll-free   1-888-232-4444 (Canada & US)
Fax   250-383-6804   E-mail   sales@trafford.com
Web site   www.trafford.com   TRAFFORD PUBLISHING IS A DIVISION OF TRAFFORD HOLDINGS LTD.
Trafford Catalogue #00-0117   www.trafford.com/robots/00-0117.html

10   9   8   7   6

ACKNOWLEDGMENTS

I am grateful to a number of people for the help they have given to me while writing this book. I particularly wish to thank the following: my wife Jean, for her creative suggestions and help in prompting my memory; Dr. Duncan Robertson and his daughter Jane, for their help in the review and editing of the original manuscript; Dr. Graham Clarkson and Dr. Clark Sharp (Edinburgh), who also helped by critically reading and commenting; Mrs. Fern Reid, for her patience and conscientious efforts on the word processor, and her diligence in interpreting my handwriting; Mrs. Ricki Kelsall, who helped out when Mrs. Reid bought a new computer which could not accommodate the old floppy disk; Bob Ashforth (Victoria), who was extremely heplful in proof reading my manuscript, and making corrections and useful comments; and finally, Derek Rennie, who challenged me to put in writing my experience and recount some anecdotes.

TABLE OF CONTENTS

Chapter

CHAPTER I

THE INITIATION

Oh dear! What can the matter be... is it an acute appendicitis or a kidney infection? My first emergency call in general practice at two o'clock in the morning. A pretty young teenager with lower abdominal pain on her right side. If it is a pyelitis, i.e., a kidney infection, the pain should be over the kidney or referred to the back or loin, but not usually to the front of the lower part of the abdomen. On the other hand, an ascending infection from the bladder can simulate appendicitis, and she had no localized acute tenderness or rigidity over the McBurney's point – this is a point of special tenderness in appendicitis and corresponds with the normal position of the appendix. In hospital it is usually quite easy to get a second opinion or to check the urine, but at 2 a.m. should I send her into hospital as an emergency?

I decided that she had a pyelitis and recommended treatment accordingly. However, niggling thoughts persisted... what if my diagnosis was wrong and she really was suffering from an acute appendicitis?

One look at the patient later that morning reassured me that my diagnosis was correct. She was sitting up in bed smiling, and told me she was "canny". What did she mean by "canny"?

To my Scottish mind the word meant astute, or cautious with money. In the North-East of England I soon learned that it usually meant "good" or "nice".

I had graduated from medical school in Glasgow a few months ago and decided to join a busy general practice with a partner and over 5000 patients in the coal-mining town of Bishop Auckland, near Newcastle-upon-Tyne.

So now I had successfully met my first emergency challenge in the new setting – but would I be accepted by the practice's regular patients? It was rather intimidating when I stopped the car in a street of row houses, occupied mainly by the families of coal miners, to see curtains moving in the windows, or doors opening so that the inhabitants could critically view the appearance and manner of the new young doctor.

Perhaps even more embarrassing was to eavesdrop on the conversations being conducted in the waiting room, or passageway in a home where we held our branch surgery.

Another test came when I was called to descend into a coal mine to treat a severely injured miner; on returning to the surface it was encouraging to be greeted by a big mug of tea, a pat on the back, and words of 'Thanks, Doc'.

My first experience of being underground had been as a child, and this had been an alarming experience. A relative, who was manager of a coal mine, had taken my father and me on a tour, and we became trapped in an airlock for about 30 minutes.

I was also about to learn the difference between deep mines and drift mines, and the different sizes of coal seams. The most uncomfortable was the twenty-inch seam where it was difficult to move; and even more difficult to treat an injured worker, something not anticipated in medical school.

Then there was the challenge of delivering babies in the home, some of which were not always accommodating in modern conveniences. Moreover, many of the patients had not experienced the benefits of a good antenatal service, which further complicated the safe delivery of the baby. In a very short space of time I became quite experienced in dealing with the complications of pregnancy and birth.

However, such conditions were not foreign to me. As final year medical students in Glasgow, we had to be innovative and ready to cope with all manner of predicaments. As part of our training in midwifery we had to accompany a trainee mid- wife on home deliveries in very poor homes and in all kinds of conditions.

For my first experience at delivering a baby we were trans- ported to the home by a regular bus; on the way I asked the nurse – for reassurance – how many babies have you deliv- ered? To my chagrin, she admitted that this was her first, and she was equally mortified on learning that I was also uniniti- ated.

When we arrived at our victim's home, we tried to act with confidence and professionalism, but this was quickly under- mined when we diagnosed twins. Our confidence was soon restored when we successfully delivered the twins and left a grateful mother with two healthy babies.

Perhaps this event had even more significance for me, as one of our supercilious lecturers had outlined the difficulties associated with the diagnosis of twins, then proceeded to as- sure us that the lady he was about to deliver had only one offspring. Having delivered the baby and placenta, he contin- ued to lecture when a second baby appeared.

We had other babies arrive in quick succession. One we delivered in a brothel. The nature of business was not appar- ent to us on our entrance to the building, but it soon became evident when I started looking for the washroom so that I could examine the placenta. On leaving the delivery room I was faced by a number of doors opening into a circular hall. The washroom wasn't visible, and a few doors had to be opened, with the inevitable interruption, before I was able to get on with my own business.

Then we had the ill fortune of trying to deliver a baby when the shilling in the gas meter ran out and left us in total darkness. It was difficult to find a shilling in these circumstances; even more difficult to find the meter. Meanwhile, the poor mother was still suffering from the birth pangs, while being told not to push and to slow down the natural process.

One experienced lady was apparently so well pleased by our ministering to her needs that, following the delivery of her tenth illegitimate baby, she asked for my name and phone number so that she could book me for delivery of the next one.

Until this time I was perhaps a little naive in assuming that most of the babies, especially those delivered to married ladies, were legitimate. This was soon dispelled after we had delivered another baby and I was completing the report form. When it came to the question, "Name of father", there was silence; the question was asked again... no reply; becoming a little exasperated, I said, "Surely you know the name of the father."

"That's the trouble," said our married lady." I don't know if it's the insurance man or the coal man". Thinking this was a joke I started to laugh, only to be brought up quickly when I realised she was in earnest.

Apart from the vicissitudes of home deliveries, we had to face the vexatious plague of fleas. So common was our little parasite that when we reported our progress to the hospital every two hours, the first item was the number of little suckers caught during our sojourn. To obtain the score, we usually resorted to the local police station where we could phone at no expense, and use the washroom where we stripped and went on a hunting spree. The count was then recorded on a blackboard, and the chief flea-catcher for the day pronounced at midnight.

This kind of infestation had some unpopular side-effects. I usually shared my hungry little surviving companions with my girl-friend and her family.

Thus while I was not without experience in obstetrics under abnormal conditions, new challenges and experiences made additional difficult and strenuous demands. Just as I was about to settle down and feel competent, we were struck by an epidemic of poliomyelitis. To add to the problems, the Medical Officer of Health published in the newspapers the early symptoms, which closely resembled colds and flu.

Needless to say, we were overwhelmed with calls, and to make matters worse, I was on my own as my partner had just left on vacation when the epidemic struck. With over 5000 patients on our list and the associated panic, it was an exhausting time.

Towards the end of the outbreak, both the local public health nurse and I succumbed to the fever. Unfortunately, the nurse developed a mild paralysis, but I escaped with an abortive attack and had to carry on without respite.

The tools for fighting infectious diseases were very limited at this time, with the main weapon being the sulphonamide drugs – commonly known as the 'M & B' – and of course, they had no effect on viral infections. They also had side-effects, and patients were advised to keep out of bright sunshine because of the risk of skin rashes. Occasionally cases were encountered in which crystals were formed in the urine and this could cause bleeding or suppression of urine so that drinking of an abundant amount of fluid was necessary. At one time it was also thought that the ingestion of sulphur in large quantities could produce toxic reactions, and patients were advised to avoid onions and eggs. Later this was considered to be unnecessary.

However, within a few years our effectiveness in treating infections improved with the introduction of other antibiotics like penicillin, streptomycin, chloromycetin, aureomycin and terramycin, and the Salk vaccine proved to be successful against polio.

By the end of my first year in general practice I began to feel

I was locked in a confined area with no opportunity to escape.

Had I made the right decision to become a physician? In fact, initially it was not my decision. My father, who was an engineer, had resolved to have at least one physician in the family, while I was equally intent on serving as a pilot in the Royal Navy Fleet Air Arm. My father's will prevailed.

Still, all was not lost. I knew that failure in three successive professional examinations ensured automatic conscription to the military. Encouraged by a school colleague, who was in a similar plight, we planned to fail our examinations. Our first challenge had the desired effect, and we happily anticipated the achievement of our primary ambition. Then my plan was abruptly derailed. The Dean of the Faculty interviewed each unsuccessful student. The resulting severe reproach I received aroused such outrage and resentment in me that I was determined to prove to the Dean that I was not a fool. Consequently I resat the examination at the end of the summer vacation and was able to continue an uninterrupted course of studies with increasing interest.

Later I discovered I could not have qualified for the Fleet Air Arm because of my medical history. I had suffered from rheumatic fever and had a heart murmur. In fact, when I graduated and believed I would belatedly join the navy, I was refused.

My school colleague was not so challenged and achieved his ambition. He died in action. The answer therefore to my question was clear. The responsibilities and trials were well compensated by the personal satisfaction of helping so many people through the problems and stress of an epidemic, as well as in the diagnosis and treatment of the variety of maladies and injuries one met in the normal general practice routine.

The preoccupation with professional demands also helped to relieve the pangs of homesickness. I had never been away from home before, and the journey south over the moors in miserable weather did not help. In addition, the mining villages and strange-sounding names like Tow Law, Houghton-le-Spring, Witton-le-Wear, Shildon, Coundon and Spennymoor tended to emphasise my remoteness from home.

Nevertheless, I was fortunate to have the comfort and support of a very kind and understanding landlady, who helped me understand the language and expectations of the people living in the area. Mrs. Soulsby had suffered severely during the war; her son had been a Battle of Britain pilot and had been shot down and killed, her husband had also been killed in the war, and her daughter's husband had been killed while flying as a bomber pilot. I was therefore adopted as a long-lost son and brother by mother and daughter. After that, I was joined by my new bride, whose support in this challenging milieu helped to bolster my resolve and ability to continue.

In addition, Jean's nursing experience was helpful when dealing with patients and assessing urgency. Sometimes by listening to their concerns and giving advice, and or a cup of tea, she would resolve the problem without the need for reference to me. We met when we were on vacation in Dunoon, a resort of the Firth of Clyde.

CHAPTER 2

"ON CALL"

It was the summer of 1946 when I moved to Bishop Auckland, County Durham, to start my career in general practice. The town was located about eleven miles from Durham City, and twenty-five miles from Newcastle-upon-Tyne. It had been the country seat of the Bishops of Durham since the 12th century, and was still the Bishop's official residence. The practice was based a few miles from the town at a village called Closehouse, which was directly adjacent to other mining villages.

The fact that one is a stranger, young, and in a respected profession, and unmarried but engaged also attracts other problems. Not that there was much time to enjoy the attractions and temptations; with only one half-day a week when I was free, and the rest of the time working or on a call, there was little time to find mischief.

I was certainly invited to some parties and met a number of people of my own age, but this was chiefly through the local church. Indeed, within a week of my arrival I was co-opted into the Church Youth Club. I wasn't sure if I could qualify but I was accepted, and it was there I met a married couple, Roy and Ivy Robertson, who have been very close friends ever since.

In any case, at the end of my first year I was married and we set up home in Leeholme, so that I could more easily cover that section of the practice. Our new home was at the end of a miners' row, or terraced housing.

OUR FIRST HOME

It had a modern bathroom but no W.C. - it was across the yard; apparently the previous owner regarded it as insanitary to have a W.C. inside a dwelling.

Indeed, the lack of sanitary conveniences was something which shocked us. Living in a city like Glasgow, we were fortunate to have a bath and other sanitary facilities. For many of the mining families, the outhouse, commonly known as "the nettie", was an earth or dry closet. The water supply was often a water tap at the middle or end of terraced housing, or at some strategic point.

Few of the mines had bathing facilities, and on return from work the miner, or perhaps more accurately, the wife filled a large tin bath, which was placed in the kitchen in front of the fire, so that he could remove the evidence of his trade. Clothes washing was equally onerous, as no electric washing machines were available.

The housing consisted of long rows of one- or two-storey buildings with backyards, at the end of which was the inevitable one- or, more friendly, two-seater dry closet.

My wife had to become accustomed to the new dialect and habits; more importantly, she had quickly to learn the districts and street names. For example, there were four "William Streets" and a duplication of many more.

For her, first time away from home, it was also a difficult time, and initially very lonely. Roy and Ivy Robertson provided some support, and my ex-landlady was a great asset.

After a few weeks my wife had a visit from a very friendly lady who invited us both one evening for supper. The amusing point about this was that the friendly lady was Mrs. Anderson, the wife of our medical competitor, and we had been warned to avoid contact with both. It need hardly be said that we became very friendly, and even more so when we befriended their new Scottish assistant and his wife, Bill and Nancy Steele.

Bill and I had the same half-day off, and we would alternate in sharing our cars for shopping or picnics. Bill had an old Morris car with a rumble or dickie seat. The lid of the boot or trunk pulled up to form the back of a seat. He inherited the car from a small neighbouring practice that his boss had purchased. On warm sunny days it was very pleasant sitting in the open seat while our wives drove; but inclement weather had the opposite effect and was embarrassing because of the wet patches we sustained on the seat of our pants, even more so when we wandered around the stores, such as Binns of Darlington.

Instead of competing in practice, we complemented one another; although I think I got the heavy end of the stick as Bill would frequently fall asleep after receiving a night call and in desperation, his patient or relative would phone me.

By this time we had been fully integrated into our community, and our interests were carefully guarded by our protective patients. One miner offered us a black Labrador retriever so that my wife would feel safe when I was out on night calls.

Unfortunately, the dog insisted on coming on call with me in the car. This I appreciated, especially in winter, as he kept the driver's seat warm until I returned.

Rationing of food was still in existence, and many of the miners had their full quota of pigs, hens, etc., plus an extra number. Consequently, when news spread that the inspectors were in the area, the extra livestock was killed and I shared in some of the surpluses. Usually there was more than we could consume, and we shared the excess with friends.

On one occasion when transporting some of the food to our friends in Bishop Auckland, we were stopped at a road-block. The police sergeant had a look inside our vehicle at the side of pork, hams, eggs, etc., then with a grin said, "Doctor, we're looking for black marketers, but, of course you wouldn't be dealing in the black market, would you?" – and with relief we drove on.

On another occasion Roy and Ivy's son was in the back seat of our car when we were transporting a side of bacon to his grandparents. The carcass was on the back seat with appropriate covering, and Duncan was unaware that he had company. As we turned a corner he put a hand out to steady himself and his hand went under the cover, to touch the cold skin. He got quite a shock! Duncan is now a physician specialising in geriatrics in Victoria, B.C.

The local magistrate was also a good friend and a patient. Quite often we would joke with one another, and if he were uncertain as to whether I was spinning a yarn or telling the truth, he would ask me to take the oath. My answer was usually, "I swear to tell the truth and **anything** but the truth." This flippancy backfired on me on one occasion when I faced him on the bench as a professional witness. While taking the oath, and without thinking, I repeated the above. Needless to say, the lawyer administering the oath was surprised and confused; my friend, with a broad grin, asked me to repeat the oath.

Patients frequently gave me tips on the local dog racing. I'm sure I could have made a fortune if I had followed their advice, and when I checked later the dog had won.

Talking of money, one of the highlights every two weeks was the counting of income from the miners' medical club. Each miner and his family paid a few shillings regularly to obtain our services. Our "collector" ensured that the payments and books were up-to-date.

This form of medical insurance was soon replaced by the National Health Service with per capita payments, i.e., each patient had to register with our practice and we received a set sum of money for each one from the government. The amount was not related to the extent of services provided; this produced an inequity between the pressures of a heavy industrial practice and the more relaxed situation in salubrious areas.

Our "collector" was not out of a job as he had other tasks, such as maintaining our dispensary where medicines were kept in concentrations of one to eight parts of water. In one practice which I looked at before moving to County Durham, the doctor had a bottle marked "Black Magic", a concoction of his own.

The practice dispensary was soon displaced by the "British National Formulary" and the local chemist. The classification of drugs was under headings like Alimentary System, Cardiovascular System and Diuretics, Respiratory System, Nervous System, etc., and contained useful notes on Emergency Treatment of Poisoning, Adverse Reactions of Drugs, etc.

The change-over also produced a few problems. The mixtures in some cases were different, although the principal ingredients were the same, but try explaining that to a patient who has been taking the same bottle regularly.

One lady, who had been paying a relatively high price for a particular mixture she had received from another physician, was very upset when she received the same mixture free through the Health Service. She was convinced it was not of the same quality nor as effective, and she couldn't be persuaded otherwise.

Also amusing was the number of patients who swore that they could not take aspirin, but asked for the little yellow tablets, which we often gave out when on our rounds. The tablets looked different, but they were aspirins.

The psychological or placebo response to drugs is well known. Later when cortisone was proclaimed as the miracle cure for arthritis, and while it was still unavailable in Britain, one of my patients obtained a supply from the U.S.A. and was treated with it. To my amazement a few weeks later this housebound lady was seen waiting for a bus and obviously participating once more in normal activities. Unfortunately, the remission did not last very long.

One prescription, which I think was matchless, was one given to me by a patient. She was a miner's wife, a spiritualist and a medium. She was crippled with chronic rheumatoid arthritis and for years she had been in a wheelchair. I visited her on a regular basis, and because of my disbelief in her conviction we frequently joked and sometimes argued about the supernatural, always on a friendly basis.

One day on my regular visit, she told me she had a message for me from an Egyptian doctor. She told me that he was my guardian and that he was anxious to pass on information to me. My response was to plead pressure of time and to pass a derogatory remark about her "spirits". She was determined, and insisted that I take out my prescription pad to record the communication. Thereafter she lapsed into a trance and, to my alarm, she rose from her wheelchair and walked round the room. She had been bound to a wheelchair for years and I was very concerned for her safety and had visions of fractures. I could only stand and stare.

I was extremely relieved when she finally collapsed into her chair. But the trance was not over. She instructed me to write down a prescription and thereupon started spelling out words, which I did not recognise. For each item she gave me a dosage, and finally instructions regarding the consumption of the mixture.

Concern changed to being wonder-struck. How could a lady, who was almost illiterate, spell out words, which at that time had no meaning to me, and to make matters more complex, give me the dosage.

Armed with this prescription, and anxious to learn if I had received some gibberish, I consulted our local chemist. After many months of research the ingredients were identified. The spelling was correct and the dosage made sense. The mixture of herbs was prepared and later consumed by the patient but without any improvement in her condition. How I regret that I did not keep a copy of the prescription.

Another phenomenon, which has an explanation, concerned a patient undergoing dental extractions. At the time I was administering anaesthetics on Saturday mornings for a local dentist. We had a regular production line; patients were ushered in by a nurse, I took the medical history and examined the patient, the anaesthetic and dental treatment were given, and then, still in a dazed condition, the patient was taken into another room. It was a sore point for me, for the dentist earned a much higher fee for each patient than I did, although I considered that my procedure carried more risk and, at the very least, equal skill.

On this occasion the lady was pregnant and had serious problems with her respiratory system. She required full extractions and her request for a general anaesthetic was refused. She remained in the dental chair and insisted that she would not leave until her wishes had been granted. Being equally adamant, I assured her that to give her an anaesthetic in her condition and in a dental chair could be tantamount to a death sentence. Still she remained in the chair, defiant. Her relatives were brought in and the problem explained to them. Their reply was: "If she wants a general anaesthetic, doctor, she has to have it!"

As a last resort to convince them of the dangers, it was decided to give them a practical demonstration. I gave the patient a whiff of the anaesthetic; as expected, she turned blue and was given oxygen. When her colour and respirations returned to normal, the mask was removed, but she didn't stir. Her reflexes were examined; she was anaesthetised! The dentist looked at me and then proceeded with the extractions. When his work was completed I tapped her on her cheek, she opened her eyes and with glee said, "I told you I could have an anaesthetic."

The explanation in this case was self-induced hypnosis. This is seen in primitive people who are highly suggestive and can perform feats like walking on live coals.

With experience I found intuition. For example one gentleman telephoned me in the middle of the night complaining that his wife was having abdominal pains, and, after a number of questions, he volunteered the opinion that "she was having her usual." As I had no intentions of turning out for a case of menstruation, he was given advice and I returned to bed.

I could not sleep, and after a few minutes got up, dressed, and drove to the patient's home. When I entered the home the husband appeared unconcerned, was preparing some tea and offered me a cup. Fortunately, I went straight into the bedroom to find his wife had collapsed in a pool of blood. She had an incomplete miscarriage and had to be rushed to hospital.

In another case, when seen, the child had severe nasal catarrh and a slight rise in temperature; he had no other symptoms or signs, so I continued on my rounds, but for no obvious reason I was still concerned about the child. I returned to his home about two hours later to find him suffering from fulminating meningococcal meningitis. He died twenty-four hours later.

In a brighter vein, a big part of my life was answering the telephone. We did not have an automatic dialling system, answering machines or cellular telephones. We had local operators who became good friends, but at times were exasperating.

When visiting friends or the cinema and on call, I would give the operator the telephone number or the name of the cinema. Consequently, he or she was soon very knowledgeable about our friends and our habits.

Even when I was not on call and a patient insisted that he or she wanted my services, the operator would phone around until I received the message. There were also embarrassing moments when we forgot to inform the operator of our return home, and our friends received an urgent call, usually in the early hours of the morning.

As far as the cinema was concerned, the managers soon became tired of flashing messages on the screen, and arrangements were made for me to phone down so that seats could be reserved. One advantage of this arrangement was that we did not have to wait in line. We also had to be accompanied by friends so that my wife could have transport home if it was necessary for me to leave before the end of the programme.

One New Year's Eve my partner contacted me, suggesting I should have a few days off to spend some time with our families in Scotland. As I did not finish my home visits until late, I had just over an hour to get to Darlington to catch the train. While I was phoning in an attempt to get a lock-up for my car at the station, the telephone operator interrupted and suggested that I should complete my preparations and he would ensure my reservation. He later phoned back to confirm the arrangements.

Saturday nights were always busy, and many calls were received to attend an emergency in the Miner's Social Club. One time, as I approached the Social Club in Closehouse, it was quite apparent that a serious problem existed. The street was crowded and the lone policeman was having difficulty in keeping the road outside the club clear.

However, as soon as my car appeared, a passage was quickly made, and I proceeded into the premises to find a miner prostrate on the floor in a pool of blood. He had a history of gastric ulcers, had been drinking heavily, and had vomited a large quantity of blood. Because of his serious condition, I accompanied him in the ambulance and my car was returned safely to my home by the union leader.

There is no doubt that the miners enjoyed the relaxation and comradeship of the Social Club, and it provided the necessary relief from the hard demands and dangers associated with their work. For the few who suffered from silicosis, a condition caused by impregnation of the lungs with silica, there was little relief for friendship or for breathing; it was heartbreaking to see a miner in the last stages of the disease.

They were very tough. One old miner who was in his late seventies was our odd-job man around the Closehouse surgery. One hot summer day things were slack and I observed old Ben simonizing my car. Feeling a bit guilty, I decided to help him, but after a few minutes of polishing I was perspiring and tired, while Ben still looked fresh and active.

The miners and their families were also very loyal and friendly. On one occasion my friend Roy used my car for an errand, and was stopped and questioned by a couple of miners, who wanted to know if he had permission to use my car. Another time, when I was still on my rounds, I was informed that my wife had a male visitor, did I know of this? A friend, who worked in West Hartlepool, had come to spend the weekend with us.

As already mentioned, dog racing was a popular sport, and one morning I was dismayed to find the waiting-room and adjoining yard packed with a motley group of men. The first patient examined had dubious signs of a back injury; then the penny dropped. It was a special day of racing, and miners required a doctor's line if they were absent, to ensure their bonus pay. To test his authenticity, the patient was informed that because of the crowded waiting-room he would be required to go home, to lie in bed until I could find time to come and examine him more thoroughly. When he realised it would be late in the day before I could see him again, he suggested with a sigh that the injury wasn't all that serious and left. The next patient had the same tale and result. Soon there was a rapid dispersion.

One area of inexperience for me was public speaking. It was therefore with some surprise that a request was received to chair a combined choir festival at the local Methodist church. Having received reasonable notice, I had my notes prepared and rehearsed so that a few days prior to the festival I was so confident that I discarded my notes. At the festival my confidence and memory completely disappeared when I stood up and was confronted by a mass of faces. From then on I had to ad lib, and I was sure my audience was not impressed. It has been said that a speech is like a birth, easy to conceive but hard to deliver. It certainly gets easier with practice, but from then on I always made certain that I retained my notes, even if I didn't have to use them.

Another mistake I made was to describe to a close friend the details of one's professional activities. Interested in the skills required to deliver a baby, and more specifically a forceps delivery, my friend Roy asked for a graphic description. I had just returned home following a forceps delivery, and proceeded to demonstrate how the forceps were used. After a few minutes into my demonstration, Roy arose and began weaving and staggering across the room. Initially we were very amused, assuming he was play-acting, but we soon realised he was not when he crashed to the floor.

Yet one more mistake was to initially ignore the diagnosis made by a patient. The lady was in her forties, had been married for many years and had no children. She came to me with symptoms generally associated with the menopause. She insisted she was pregnant. Her menstruation had stopped, she had no history of morning sickness but she did complain of a sense of increased fullness of her breasts. This latter symptom I put down to an excessive desire to have a child before she was too old.

When she returned a few weeks later with her mother, both insisting on pregnancy, I examined her and found her to be about three months pregnant. I later delivered the baby, and whenever the child needed to be seen, the mother would, with a smile and a mischievous look in her eyes, ask me to examine her menopause.

Following three years in the practice, I had a serious disagreement with my partner over some aspects of the practice administration and emergency cover.

We were not able to resolve our problems and reluctantly I was forced to look elsewhere. It was with considerable sadness that we said farewell to our friends and patients. In spite of the pressure of work, we had formed very strong and emotional bonds with the people in our area; it was almost like leaving home again.

CHAPTER 3

TRULY RURAL

My new practice was centred in a village in Ayrshire, Scotland, called Tarbolton. The compact mining villages around Bishop Auckland contrasted with the scattered villages and the surrounding beauty of the countryside of my new district, which masked the hard realities and demands imposed by distance. A considerable amount of travel was required, and it was difficult to organise and time visits. For example, one could set out after morning surgery with a small list of visits for Symington, which was about five to six miles from base, only to find when you got there that many more people wished you to visit them. Thus you finished up returning home for lunch well after the normal time.

To make matters worse, visits to a particular village could be interrupted if an emergency call was received from the other end of the practice. For those who know the district, the practice covered a wide area from the outskirts of Mauchline to the suburbs of the town of Ayr, to Moncton, Symington, Mossblown and Annbank.

The land was very fertile; farming was the principal industry, with a coal mine at Mossblown. The mine in this case was a deep mine with long, wide avenues; transportation underground was frequently required.

Contact in an emergency could be a serious problem. One farmer's wife who went into premature labour was such a case. The husband and ultimately the police tried to contact my partner and me as we travelled across the countryside.

I eventually received the call and proceeded along a winding and undulating road at speed. As I ascended a rise in the road, the farmer and the policeman could be seen walking back and forth in the yard, obviously in a very agitated state. On my arrival their relief was unmistakable, but on entering the home my mood changed to one of alarm. The mother was lying uncovered and unconscious in the bed, the new-born baby was lying face down in a pool of amniotic fluid, and the mother-in-law and servant girl were in hysterics.

A quick examination of the mother revealed no evidence of severe haemorrhage and I assumed that she had fainted. The baby, however, was a more serious problem and attempts were immediately made at resuscitation. Fortunately, the response was quite rapid. Thereafter the mother-in-law and maid had to be calmed so that they could take care of the baby. The mother was revived, and the storm and stress were replaced with smiles and the cries of a healthy baby; for me there was much relief that the situation had a happy ending.

Why did the husband or police fail to phone for an ambulance? Their answer was that the labour was progressing rapidly, this was not her first, and they were afraid the baby would be born in the ambulance. What surprised me more in this case was the fact that no one had attempted to tend to the infant's needs, and they panicked in a farming family well used to the birth process.

Of course, not infrequently the emergency turns out to be frivolous. One gentleman called me at three o'clock on a very cold and frosty morning. The need for the call was vague and difficult to understand as I had visited him in his home the previous day; he was recovering from a mild attack of influenza. The neighbour, who was telephoning on his behalf, insisted that he was very ill but failed to provide any more evidence. Reluctantly I agreed to respond. When seen, the man was sitting in front of a blazing coal fire reading a book. Asked how his condition had changed from my very recent visit, his reply was to the effect that he was very constipated, he was worried that he had not had a movement for a week. My irate response and advice ensured that he never again consulted me about that condition.

Sometimes the emergency is more tragic and distressful. One lady was standing at a tradesman's van on a straight part of the road when she was struck by another vehicle. She suffered multiple fractures and internal damage. She was rushed to hospital but died soon after. At the scene of the accident, and just before the victim was removed by ambulance, the husband questioned me about the possibility of financial compensation.

Occasionally an emergency can cause embarrassment. Such a predicament occurred when a lady, who was an epileptic, collapsed in the street. She was renowned in the village for her licentious behaviour, and was reputed to have run down the street after the paper-boy because he had failed to pay her for services rendered.

One day as I cruised towards home and turned a corner, the brakes had to be slammed on because of a body lying in the middle of the road. She had had an epileptic fit and was still in a state of stupor; she had to be carried into the car. When we arrived at her home she was still very drowsy and kept pawing me, possibly a form of post-epileptic automatism, but the neighbours could have had a different interpretation. In any case, I was very relieved when she returned to her family.

Another embarrassing situation was experienced when visiting the home of a local artist. Displayed around the walls of her room were pictures of the most erotic and explicit sex scenes. I am not a prude, but considered the artwork inappropriate for the children I was examining.

In yet another case, when calling at the home of a miner and his family to examine their small son, I found the door ajar and mother and father were having a very heated argument using a great variety of swear words. It took a number of knocks on the door terminating in a loud shout of "Doctor" before they realised I was in the room. The mood immediately changed, I proceeded to examine the child and, in due course, he repeated several of the swear words with equal emphasis; his mother with the most angelic smile said, "Doctor, I don't know where he picked up these awful words, he never hears it in this house."

In practice one gets used to many odours, but in this case I was extremely relieved to escape outdoors. The cottage was situated on a hillside overlooking a lush valley with cattle grazing and lazily enjoying the hot sunshine. The white of the cottage contrasted with a background of trees and shrubs, idyllic on the outside, but repugnant inside. The temperature outside was high, but inside it was much higher due to the efforts of a well stoked fire. A rope criss-crossed the room and on it hung various garments soaked in urine. The patient, a woman in her late thirties, was incontinent and lay on top of a urine-soaked mattress. The blankets and the patient's night-dress had also been contaminated; the medical history and examination had to be completed quickly.

This practice provided an excellent antenatal service, although initially I must admit to some annoyance at having to fill clinical forms in triplicate. Another bureaucratic procedure for the filing cabinets. One copy was sent to the hospital, one to the local midwife, and one for my own records. I was soon disillusioned when, a few weeks after one of my early clinics, the hospital obstetrician phoned me to enquire if I would like a patient with the early signs of pre-eclamptic toxaemia (slight rise in blood pressure, increase in weight over five pounds per month, etc.) admitted to hospital. In this case treatment had been started and we decided to keep the lady at home; but I received the promise of a bed should this become necessary.

The hospital's department of obstetrics had a team of specialists on twenty-four-hour call with a specially equipped ambulance, which could be rushed at a moment's notice in a case of emergency. The hospital was located in the town of Irvine, about 12 miles north-west of Tarbolton.

I was very happy to use this service when called to a patient who had kept her pregnancy secret, had had no medical attention, and delivered the baby with the help of a friend. Unfortunately, she had a post-partum haemorrhage and I had to struggle to keep her alive. The emergency team arrived in record time from Irvine, and they quickly had control.

Our first child was born when we were living in Tarbolton. We engaged my university professor in Glasgow for the antenatal care and delivery, at the same time booking a bed in the nursing home. Glasgow was about thirty miles from our home. In the late weeks of my wife's pregnancy she was found to have a breech presentation. This was corrected, but my professor caused us some concern when he told us he was going on vacation but hoped to be back in time for the birth. "What if the fetus resumes the old presentation?" His answer was that he had every confidence in my ability to repeat an external version, but if I had any concerns to contact his assistant. I didn't feel too happy, but in the end I had to repeat the correction. The labour pains started soon after we bade farewell to relatives who had spent the weekend with us. My wife was assured that it would take some time, as this was her first pregnancy. So we went to bed.

Sleep was periodically disturbed and reassurance given, but eventually I was persuaded to do more than comfort. On examination, I found my wife's labour was advancing; the cervix was dilating. So at six o'clock in the morning she was bundled into the car and off we rushed to the nursing home. By the time we reached the nursing home the labour pains were not so frequent, and it wasn't until 8 p.m. that I received the good news that we had a daughter.

The new baby, Aileen, created a lot of interest and advice. Our partner's wife had a housekeeper who had many sons but no daughters; she was on our doorstep to receive the new baby, and was a frequent visitor. My partner's wife had advised my wife that our black Labrador might be jealous of the new baby; in any case it was wise to keep him apart because of the possibility of spreading disease. A few hours following their return, my wife and I were having tea with Mrs. Dunlop, the housekeeper, when we missed the dog, and went out to check on the baby and the dog.

The baby was lying in her carry-cot on top of the chesterfield in the living room; the dog was standing beside her licking her face and her hands. From then on the dog was her guardian and her constant companion. In fact on one occasion at a later date, we were very alarmed to find our daughter's faeces were black, and immediately thought of the worst possible causes. Fortunately, before we had a chance to start an investigation, we found she had been sharing the dog biscuits with the Lab, and it was the charcoal biscuits which were the culprit.

One of the hazards of operating in a farming region is the approach to the farm building, to open and shut gates, and occasionally to face inquisitive and/or aggressive animals. At one farm I complained to the farmer about his bull; he responded by extolling the virtues of this animal. Not long afterwards an emergency call was received when he was gored by his virtuous bull.

The village of Tarbolton was known for its connection with the Scottish poet Robert Burns, particularly the Bachelor's Club. This Club was still operating and had a very active literary society.

The village also had a local bard, an eighty-year-old, Allan Carswell, who had quite a varied life. He had been a sailor on

old sailing ships, a farmer in South Africa, and was still thatch-
ing local houses. Twice a year this poet produced poems; the
first was received with trepidation as it summarised events in
the village, including the scandals. The second reviewed the
efforts of speakers at the literary society, and some of his comments were not always complimentary.

I was privileged to give a paper on psychology at the request of the society. Much to my relief my efforts were given
favourable comments. Part of the digest, I thought, most amusing and worth repeating:

> "The Doctor had foundation in his science,
> Seemed grafted on some reliance;
> The object is so plain,
> To open up the sluggish cells
> And make them click again.
>
> When some little boy at school
> Seems to drop and fall behind,
> We are apt to say you little fool
> When it's really a faulty tool.
> It could be rightened, who can tell;
> Psychology may find the cell that sticks
> With scientific treatment, get the cell to tick.
>
> I think of my school days
> That are past and gone,
> Had the Science functioned then,
> I might have been a don."

Social life was very limited because of the pressure of work
and Tarbolton's population was just over 500. Consequently
we depended on visits from friends and relatives. One night
we were awakened by a loud bang and ran out from the bedroom. At first there was no evidence as to the cause, then we

saw thick white dust seeping from under one of the bedroom doors. On opening the door we encountered a white fog; once we were able to penetrate the fog we found that the lath and plaster ceiling had collapsed, and covered by a mass of plaster and lath my father-in-law lay uninjured – still sound asleep, and quite oblivious of the catastrophe.

As junior partner, I was expected to take the majority of night calls, and my only half-day release from duty was frequently interrupted if we stayed at home.

The house we owned had no front garden, and house and garage presented a continuous obstacle. At first we thought that by locking the front door we would be free from prying eyes and calls. Yet patients frequently circumvented this obstacle by walking into our neighbour's garden and calling over the fence. Even when we visited our relatives or friends in Glasgow, it was not unusual to find patients waiting at the front door for my return.

Eventually with the stress of working seven days a week, emergency work with disturbed sleep, irregular meals and relentless telephone calls, my health began to suffer. On a visit to Glasgow, after a very stressful day, I was having supper when I suddenly had an urgent desire to visit the toilet. To my distress, I discovered that a considerable amount of blood had been passed. On returning to the dining table, I made an excuse that we should return home, and then drove the thirty miles back to Tarbolton.

When we reached home I informed my wife of the real reason for our abrupt departure and immediately retired to bed. In the middle of the night I awoke with a feeling of dizziness, and again the urgent desire to defecate. I jumped out of bed, but collapsed on the way to the bathroom.

To complicate matters, I had phoned my partner to inform him that I had suffered a rectal haemorrhage, and asked him to cover for emergencies. As a result, our telephone was switched off, and my wife had to run to our neighbour and had difficulty in rousing them to phone for an ambulance.

My next recollection was regaining consciousness in Ayr County Hospital. As my senses returned I could discern, at first vaguely, a figure in a white coat. It was a man, he smiled, then confused me by saying, "You have talked to me often, we have corresponded regularly, but you have never met me personally, I am Dr. DeSoldenov, obstetrician and gynaecologist from Irvine Central Hospital."

"Oh, it's Bolshy!"

He laughed and said, "Yes, Bolshy; I've just come to wish you well and to apologise."

"Apologise for what?"

"Well, I'm very sorry I cannot use my expertise to help you recover; as you know I don't treat your kind of haemorrhage. As a recompense, and to keep your mind off your problem, I have brought you some reading material."

At the side of my bed was a pile of "Playboy" or similar magazines.

Following intensive investigation, no definite cause could be found for my symptoms and I was transferred to Glasgow Royal Infirmary for more investigation. By this time I was feeling very well, but amused to find I was being admitted to the ward where I had been a houseman. A number of the staff were still known to me. I was put in the "death bed", i.e., the bed next to the duty room, so that I could sign the various orders and forms.

Not long after my admission I decided to play a prank on the staff. In those days the food was brought in trolleys to the duty room and the nurses had to dish out the food. While they were occupied with their task I strolled in and emptied a syphon of soda-water on them.

A few days later, I was passing the time by playing cards with some of the patients when my old chief walked in for a ward round. We had all to jump back into bed; when I attempted to get into bed I found that the nurses had made an "apple-pie" bed so that I had to lie hunched with my knees bent. To the staff nurse standing at my bed-side, I threatened severe retribution, but she reacted by soaking me with soda-water.

Senior medical staff do not usually accept with equanimity the pranks of junior staff, and lying there in a soggy and awkward position, I was certain my old chief would not be amused, especially as the expected abdominal examination would be out of the question. On such occasions one has to be resource-ful; at this time it was fortunate that the open golf champion-ship was being played. My chief was an ardent golfer, so that a discussion about the players and golf scores took his mind off my condition and avoided a crisis.

It was a change to experience life at the other end of a hospi-tal bed. It gave me a different perspective and made me aware of the sensitivity of a patient when his or her case is being discussed. It is very easy to misinterpret, particularly when one attempts to eavesdrop.

As for my own condition, at first it was thought that the haemorrhage was caused by a polyp in the bowel, but eventu-ally the diagnosis was haemorrhagic duodenitis, and it was recommended that I should be on a diet and be more regular with my meals. To-day this would have been diagnosed as an acute duodenal ulcer and cured with antibiotics and other medi-cations to suppress acid secretion.

On return to practice it was impossible for me to abide by the recommended regime, and about a year later I had a mild recurrence. This time my partner arranged for me to see an-other specialist at Glasgow's Western General Hospital. He confirmed the previous diagnosis.

At this stage a decision had to be taken on whether to re-main in general practice or to make a change. Thoughts of industrial or rehabilitative medicine had been considered. Be-cause of my experience I had been concerned about the results of prolonged disability due to an accident. It was very noticeable, even in my relatively short period of practice, that when a healthy and hard-working miner or farm worker was unable to work for over three months, he appeared to lose his pride and zest for returning to work.

Thus the decision was made in the summer of 1952 to return to the university to take a Diploma in Industrial Medicine and the Diploma in Public Health. The year this decision was made, the university dropped the former and I took the Diploma in Public Health, which was still acceptable for work in the field of industrial medicine.

It was a period of economic stress as no income was received, nor were grants available for the university course, so that we had to dig into savings and live with our in-laws. In addition, one had to become a student again; I had a shock when given a statistical exercise which necessitated the use of logarithms – I had forgotten how to use the tables. When I approached some friends who were teachers, I was even more frustrated until we found one who was a mathematician.

CHAPTER 4

A PERIOD OF ORIENTATION

In 1953, with my new diploma in hand, a search for a suitable appointment became a priority. There were few openings for industrial appointments, and to fill time and of course to pay bills, a public health position was applied for.

The position was in the town of Middlesborough, and here I met a remarkable man, Dr. E.C. Downer, the Medical Officer of Health (M.O.H.), who was a very competent administrator, an excellent teacher, and a linguist, speaking the colloquial as well as the accepted; he also had great empathy and a wonderful sense of humour.

Just prior to my interview with the Council, Dr. Downer warned me to ask if the Authority would pay me the new salary scales, which had recently been approved for Assistant Medical Officers. What he failed to tell me at the time was that the position for which I was applying had been downgraded from Senior Medical Officer to the Assistant level to save money.

Consequently, when I started work in the department it was rather disconcerting to find my duties were next to the deputy, Dr. Bob Taylor, and over other physicians who had been in the service for some time. Besides this, a short time after my appointment the deputy went on vacation and a few days later, Dr. Downer took ill and had to be admitted to hospital.

Soon after, a summons was received to visit Dr. Downer and he thereupon discussed the three options he saw open to him. First, he could call the deputy back from his holiday; secondly, he could attempt to run the department from his hospital bed; and lastly, he could have me assume the responsibility with the option to consult with him when I deemed it necessary.

We decided that I should be in charge. Fortunately we had other experienced administrative staff who gave me every assistance. But this change of events meant that the breadth of my experience was rapidly extended, and, instead of writing letters and reports in longhand, I had to dictate directly to our typist. It also meant meeting many more of the staff than was normal for my position. Regular meetings in hospital with Dr. Downer kept him informed, and his advice encouraged me to continue.

Happily, I came through that experience unscathed, and my next lessons were in handling correspondence associated with difficult or problem cases, and the writing of submissions and strategy when making requests to Council.

A letter had been received from a father who was seeking custody of his handicapped child. The mother was providing good care, but in the divorce proceedings the father claimed that this was not so. He was a lawyer and accused the department of incompetence, and of making false statements in support of the mother. His evidence was equally a sham.

I was incensed on reading the letter, and drafted a reply that I thought was appropriate. Dr. Downer scanned most of the letters leaving the department and called me to his office. We reviewed the letter and my reply. He sympathised with my reaction, then asked what kind of reply my letter would evoke. I assumed the rhetoric would go on for some time and probably become even more aggressive. How would this appear if the correspondence were produced in court, was his next question. I had to admit that it could be damaging to our case.

Then he gave me advice, which I have always found to be very useful and effective. He told me that when one becomes involved in a contentious situation, don't express opinions, stick to the facts, as these are indisputable. In this case a factual letter would irritate the father, who was a lawyer and would most likely continue his unfounded allegations. Dr. Downer continued: provided your replies remain factual, this father would be viewed as unreasonable and unfit to assume custody of the child. This is exactly what happened. Likewise, preparing a submission for Council was, for Dr. Downer, like playing a game of chess. Each player or Council member would react according to the perceived challenge. An informed knowledge of the players' interests and idiosyncrasies ensured fairly accurate anticipation of the outcome. But the setting and wording had to be designed to provoke the right reaction. For example, if the report initiated a negative response from the opposition, and the ruling members could see some political gain, the desired decision was obtained.

It was therefore very enlightening and amusing to sit at a Council meeting and observe the game of chess played out exactly as planned.

Later in my career, especially if I thought the outcome was vital to the success of the service, and sometimes with a critical rehearsal with my staff, we deployed these techniques with success. Administrative wrangling with the heads of other departments could also be resolved by self-control, patient analysis of the reasons for contention, followed by diplomatic discussions, sometimes in the bar or over a luncheon meeting. Dr. Downer's view was that most issues could be resolved over a glass of beer.

Evidence of his self-control and humour can best be illustrated by the following incident. We were walking through the entrance hall to the department when we saw a very angry man pacing back and forth in front of reception. The man was approached and asked if we could help. After shouting a few angry words, the man said he wanted "to see the bloody M.O.H. and to give him a piece of his mind". With a smile, he was quietly told that the M.O.H. had an appointment, but if he came upstairs to the office we would attempt to arrange an interview. On the way up the man continued with his crude diatribe, was shown into the outer office and Dr. Downer's secretary told that the man was wanting an interview with the M.O.H. Dr. Downer then entered his own office through another door and informed his secretary he would see the man. Needless to say, the gentleman was somewhat dumbfounded.

One of the duties of the department was Port Medical Authority. We had a number of port health inspectors and our own launch so that the ships, incoming food and passengers could be inspected. On warm sunny days it was sometimes a pleasant relief to accompany the inspectors at their work. The deputy and I provided a twenty-four-hour emergency cover, and shared with the M.O.H. the routine review of port-related health issues.

When we boarded a ship we were always escorted to the captain's day cabin and served drinks. Initially this was unsettling for me as I did not drink alcohol, and refusal was met with disbelief. In fact, a few of the captains construed my refusal as a joke, and recognising my Scottish accent, proceeded to provide me with a large glass of our native brew. In these cases one had to find places to get rid of the contents. Finally I found that the best way out was to ask for a light beer.

One Italian captain made the unfortunate mistake of assuming his language was unknown to his visitors. On this occasion I accompanied my chief and we had the usual refreshments. After we had completed our business we were accompanied to the gangway by the captain and his first officer. As we disembarked, my chief said something in Italian which caused them to blush and to look flustered. When I questioned the reason for their reaction, Dr. Downer informed me that when he had asked for a beer, the captain said, "Get this big fat bugger a beer." My chief had thanked them in Italian for the beer, "even though they considered him to be a big fat bugger."

Especially memorable was one medical emergency we answered at the port. A call was received in the middle of a cold winter night. The ship, carrying iron ore, was moored at a most inaccessible place in the port. We had to walk quite a distance over railway lines, avoiding shunting engines and rolling stock, with our heads lowered to brace ourselves against the cold wind and rain.

Once on board, we found that the "emergency" was a sailor suffering from mumps. In the crowded conditions prevailing in the ship it was impossible to isolate him. At the same time I did not feel the need to immediately transfer him to the hospital, and arranged for this later in the morning.

Just as we were about to disembark, the captain suggested that I should perhaps examine another member of the crew who had taken ill the day before. In the captain's words, "He had probably eaten something which had disagreed with him as he had abdominal pain and had vomited." We proceeded back down to the crew's quarters to find a man with acute abdominal pains and marked abdominal rigidity. It was evident that he had an acute appendicitis, which had perforated.

How were we to get him to the hospital? An ambulance could not get near the ship, and to carry him on a stretcher over the route we had taken in the prevailing conditions would be very hazardous.

We decided to use our launch, which was equipped for ambulance cases. We rushed back to find our launch moored between two other vessels. With some difficulty, and with the help of my port health inspector who was more experienced in handling these situations, we sailed down river to the ship.

It was low tide and we just had enough water to get alongside. In poor light we had then to ascend and descend a rope ladder brushing against the barnacles and slime of the exposed hull. To add to our frustration and to our patient's peril, the ropes the crew attached to our stretcher were several feet too short. In the darkness and with language difficulties, we couldn't get the Greek sailors to understand the problem. In the end we had to leave the patient dangling while I quickly went up the ladder again, then descended so that I could help the port inspector manoeuvre the patient into the warmth and safety of the cabin. Miraculously, the patient survived the ordeal.

The sleazy side of seaports is well known, and on one occasion during a visit with the police I sat in the car while the policeman and policewoman elaborated on their extensive knowledge of passers-by. At this time our concern was a very obese prostitute who operated from her own home. She had a number of syphilitic ulcers on her legs and was a chronic source of infection. She had to be helped by her husband to bed when customers arrived. He also collected the fee for service.

We had no power under the Public Health Act to forcibly remove this woman for treatment. The police could probably have charged her with keeping a bawdy-house but this would have had very limited effect. We therefore concocted a plan of bluff and persuasion.

I visited the lady and her husband, and made every effort to persuade them that she urgently needed treatment. They reacted by pleading loss of income and denied the need for treatment. When I suggested that they could lose their income if the police charged them with operating a house of prostitution, and noted the presence of a police car in the street, they finally agreed. The ambulance service and the hospital had been forewarned, so that as soon as my call was received they responded rapidly to prevent a change of heart.

We had a public health nurse who followed up on contacts of venereal disease, now called sexually transmitted diseases.

At first she was dressed in the regular public health nurse uniform, but she was recognised for her responsibilities and referred to as "Syphie Sue". She then changed into civilian dress, but this did not change her label.

Life in a seaport was also of interest to an Anglican convention in London about this time, and my chief was asked to give a paper on the subject. His address aroused so much interest that for two Sundays the papers published accounts of his speech. In one newspaper the first issue noted that he was a bachelor, and in the second one, that he had a son. The natural reaction of readers and probable intention of the newspaper was to assume that the son was illegitimate, but in fact, he had adopted the boy and reared him as his own son when very close friends were killed in a road accident.

In any case, the result of this publicity was an immense amount of mail, with many proposals of marriage or companionship, and in some cases, very lewd language and explicit pictures. It was a period when the review of the morning mail was far removed from dull routine.

Dr. Downer's fondness for children and his kindness were clearly evident to us on our first Christmas in Middlesborough. Early that morning he appeared with a gift for our two-year-old daughter, and spent over an hour entertaining and being entertained by her.

At the other end of the age scale was a lady in her late seventies who sold newspapers at the railway station every day. Many appeals were made to the department by concerned commuters who deplored the fact that this dear old lady had to sit in all kinds of weather to sell newspapers. I was asked to talk to her and eventually she agreed to "retire". Until then she regularly took out two books from the library, but the day after she left her post she handed her books in and took none out. The next day she was found dead. She did not commit suicide, merely lost interest in living. This experience certainly made me much more sensitive to the needs of the elderly.

In Middlesborough I saw my first and only case of scurvy. It is rarely seen in the Western world, and is caused by vitamin C deficiency. A request had been made for help for a disabled person. When I visited the home there was no response at first and growing impatient, I looked through the letter-box. I saw a thin, very pale man walking with a peculiar gait and with swellings in his legs. When he opened the door he was having some difficulty in breathing, and I noted that the swellings in his legs were due to haemorrhages. My first conclusion was that he had been the victim of abuse, but further examination and the condition of his gums confirmed the diagnosis of scurvy. He was in his early thirties, living alone and obviously neglecting his diet.

A considerable amount of my work was concentrated on the handicapped and community care of the mentally ill. Surveys and plans had to be developed; contact and working arrangements with the voluntary associations were also encouraged. Little did I realise that this interest and experience would greatly influence my future career.

About this time my brother-in-law, who worked for the Colonial Service in Kenya, was home on a visit and he tried to persuade me to make a change. In the end I yielded to his arguments and submitted an application for a post in Uganda.

In due course a reply was received inviting me for an interview at the Colonial Office in London. The interview was conducted by a senior civil servant and a doctor, whose role appeared to be subservient.

An explanation was given of the responsibilities of the post. When I was told that these included a 400-bed general hospital and that major surgery would be conducted by me, I protested. I was not a surgeon. "Surely you are qualified in surgery?" asked the interviewer. "Yes, as part of my general degree, but that does not qualify me to undertake major surgical operations. I would need further training."

For the next several minutes we argued about this until the

doctor intervened in support of my stand. After some more discussion, it was pointed out that a bungalow was not immediately available for me and my family, that they would have to follow me at a later date. I didn't think this would be a problem, suggesting that my family could travel to Kenya to join my sister-in-law and her husband until a bungalow was accessible. However, it became impossible to convince this civil servant that this was a reasonable request. Following some more contention, and feeling very angry and frustrated, I told him, in no uncertain terms, that I wasn't interested. To my amazement, some weeks later I received a letter offering me the appointment with travel arrangements, etc.

It was, however, time to move on, although it was not without serious regrets, but necessary for my future career. We had enjoyed living in the town, it was relatively close to our very good friends in Bishop Auckland, and from a professional point of view it had been most instructive. I was indeed lucky to have started my new career under a very talented and understanding leader.

CHAPTER 5

A NEW AREA OF CHALLENGE

When a successful application for a new post is achieved, there is usually a sense of elation and excitement over the new challenge. Seldom are there any doubts, but after the news was conveyed to me by the clerk of the Council, I wondered how we would occupy our time when not working. What could we possibly do in this picturesque small town?

It is true that my last practice was in a rural district, but then the work severely limited the opportunity for social intercourse. We also had friends and relatives within a reasonable distance. Moreover, both my wife and I were used to the big city.

Situated in North-East England, the market town of Alnwick had been a border stronghold, which had survived many battles; it was dominated by Alnwick Castle, the home of the Duke and Duchess of Northumberland. The Duke's family had owned it from about the middle of the 18th century, and now it was partly a residence for the Duke and his family, and partly a training college for teachers.

Another notable feature of the town was the Hotspur Tower, the only survivor of the original four gates. Traffic had to pass through it in single file to enter or exit the main business area.

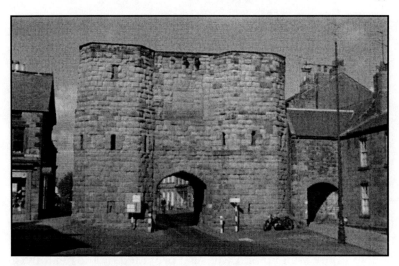

HOTSPUR TOWER

Alnwick town had just under 8000 inhabitants, and as Area
Medical Officer, I was responsible for the public health services and the Northumberland County Health Services serving Alnwick Urban and Rural Districts, Amble Urban District,
Rothbury Rural District, Glendale Rural District, Norham Rural District; and later Belford Rural District and the Borough of
Berwick-upon-Tweed were included, i.e., in 1956. I assumed
the position in 1955.

Sympathies with the English and/or Scottish interests were
quite active in the border country, and I found Berwick to be
staunchly pro-Scottish in outlook, although it was in England.
In fact, Berwick held out for some time against Northumberland
County's directive to dispense with their part-time M.O.H.
and to accept me. Under protest, they finally agreed, but made
it abundantly clear that I was acceptable only because of my
Scottish background.

Until my appointment, all the Councils were served by local
general practitioners, who were consulted on a part-time basis
on public health issues. There was no Public Health Office and
my first task was to establish an Area Health Office.

The Alnwick Urban District Council was gracious in providing accommodation adjoining the Council office. While this was being modified and refurbished, a start was made to finding staff and training them. The address of my new office was in Wagonway Road, which I thought appropriate in view of the amount of travel envisaged.

It was natural that my medical colleagues in the area were suspicious, if not resentful about my appointment. Fortunately, Alnwick had a small infirmary and maternity home, and I was able to meet frequently with them in their common room over coffee. In other districts, arrangements were made for meetings according to the availability of mutually convenient places. Help in my assimilation was also provided by the health visitors and local public health inspectors.

An additional aid was the transfer of control from Newcastle of services such as clinics, county midwifery services, health visiting, home nursing, sick-room equipment, domestic help services, ambulance services, mental health and school health services. I was also the area spokesman for health issues at the County Health Department in Newcastle on a regular basis.

Another advantage of the new direction was the ability of the public health officers from the scattered area to come together at meetings, which I held on a regular basis. In this way I was kept informed, they were able to share their experiences and problems, and we were able to adopt common policies.

As for the social side, my fears were soon banished. Within a week I was attending the Rotary Club, first as a guest, and soon after as a full member. Because of our remoteness from Newcastle, we had difficulty in obtaining speakers, and sometimes they failed to turn up.

Until this time I was very nervous about public speaking, especially after my disastrous experience at the choir festival. This soon changed, as it was common to feel a hand on your shoulder and to be told you are the speaker for this meeting.

My wife was also enrolled in the Inner Wheel and involved

in its many activities. One thing they did each year was to put on a play or concert for charity, and to entertain the elderly. They were always very successful. I was coerced on one occasion to help out when one of the ladies had to drop out at the last moment. No one else would volunteer, as there was so little time to learn the script. Fortunately, the act was that of a photographer, using one of those big old-fashioned cameras with a cover. It was possible to rig copies of the script inside the camera with a light so that just before I had to speak, it was possible to read the line from the hideout.

The Church also provided us support; shortly after we attended a service, the Minister, the Rev. Roy Backhouse, introduced us to a number of our neighbours, who were also members of his congregation.

In a very short time we had a full calendar. Just to complete the picture, I became involved with the local voluntary associations as Secretary of the Tuberculosis After-care Association, and Secretary of the Alnwick and District Old Peoples Welfare Committee!

Then one night I was late in attending a meeting of the "League of Friends of the Alnwick Infirmary". When I entered the room I was immediately escorted to the chair. Apparently the committee members could not agree on a chairman, then someone suggested that the next person to enter the room would be the chairman. Thus I assumed the position for a few years.

My area included Holy Island, which for centuries was called Lindisfarne; it lies about a mile off the Northumberland coast. It has links with two Saints, St. Aidan and St. Cuthbert. On the south-east corner of the island, Lindisfarne Castle occupies a commanding position. Nearby are the Farne Islands, famous for the rescue of shipwreck survivors by Grace Darling and her father in 1838.

Just before my first visit to Holy Island, my public health inspector counselled me about what I should expect on my visit. At that time there was no causeway; one had to depend on taxis, old T Fords that transported fee-paying passengers across the sands at low tide. I was told that after parking my car, and soon after entering the taxi, it would suddenly be crammed with islanders who would just as quickly disappear when we reached the island. These words proved to be correct.

When the causeway was completed I thought it would be a happy alternative, but there were times when one misjudged tides or almost wandered off because of mist; these were times when the experienced taxi-driver would have been an asset.

The island also appeared to have a mysterious method of warning signals. Like the Scottish island, featured in the film "Whisky Galore", when the excise men were unable to trace the whisky rescued from a shipwreck, Holy Island was also immune from sudden unwanted attention. For some time I suspected islanders were illegally collecting mussels from a bed which was contaminated by sewage. On several occasions, without informing anyone, I would veer off the highway and speed across the causeway, only to be met by a small deputation. The police had similar problems with the pubs and licensing hours.

Sewage and water supplies were other major problems in the area. One small mining community of approximately 500 people, called Radcliffe, hit the headlines when the Rural District Council asked the villagers to stop using earth closets. Instead, the Council proposed to install new chemical buckets, and according to the newspaper report the villagers protested that they urgently needed adequate water and sewage facilities, and that, in any case, the chemical buckets couldn't be fitted under the wooden seats.

In another village, sewage was discharged into a culvert and diverted by a weir and pipe before reaching the river. In the summer the pipe was often blocked, so that the sewage was trapped among reeds and became a danger to the health of the residents.

Providentially, most of the councils in my area embarked on ambitious programmes to provide adequate sewage disposal and/or to upgrade existing plants. At the same time there was a serious drive to encourage home improvements and to link them to the new plants.

These improvements were welcomed by the Duke and Duchess of Northumberland; they launched an extensive modernisation of their farms and other properties on their estate.

NORTHUMBERLAND GAZETTE, FRIDAY, OCTOBER 24, 1958

Duchess opens Cafe Chantant

The Duchess of Northumberland who opened the cafe chantant, held by the League of Friends in the Northumberland Hall, Alnwick, on Friday, making a purchase at one of the stalls from Mrs. J. Murray Lock. Looking on are Dr. R. Short and Mr. R. Hutchinson.

The Duchess took an active part in the management of the estate. On a few occasions I would meet her by chance when she was in the candy shop owned by Mrs. Leath, chairperson for the Council. When this happened we would retire to the back room to discuss her concerns or to provide information over a cup of coffee. In case there is a suggestion that we were being influenced, this was not the case as the estate was located in the rural district; Mrs. Leath represented the urban district.

The Duke amd Duchess also played an active role in other events within the district. Nineteen fifty-eight was the "Golden Jubilee" of Alnwick Infirmary and the Duke participated in

A telephone trolley was presented to Alnwick Infirmary by the League of Friends on Sunday, and here the Duchess of Northumberland is handing the receiver to the first patient to make use of it, Mrs. I. J. Geggie, of Abbeylands, while Dr. R. Short (chairman of the League of Friends) put the money in the box.

the celebrations. At that time, as chairman of the League of Friends, I was able to present a trolley telephone to the infirmary.

The Duke's mother also helped in public events. When a public meeting was organised, it was always possible to ensure a good attendance by inviting the Dowager Duchess. She lived in Lesbury village, which was about five miles from Alnwick. She had a faithful following, which helped pack the meeting hall, and many of them went back to the Dowager's home for tea after the meeting.

Plans for sewerage and water supplies brought us to another ancestral home. Accompanied by my public health inspector and surveyor, we called on the Earl of Tankerville, in Chillingham.

According to "The King's England" Northumberland, published by Hodder and Stoughton, Chillingham Castle is the best example in Northumberland of a 14th century County and Corner Turreted house. Chillingham Park is famous for its herd of wild white cattle. They were the sole survivors of their species.

The Earl opened the door and escorted us to his office where his manager awaited. After we spent some time poring over plans, the office door opened and a lady appeared with silver tray, teapot and biscuits. She then poured out the tea, and to my surprise, poured herself a cup of tea and joined us. My immediate reaction was, "How could a maid have the effrontery to join us in our tea break!" Then I realised that the "maid" was the Countess of Tankerville.

Later I met the Countess when carrying out medical examinations at the village school. The nurse reported that the Countess was in the waiting-room and asked if we should give her priority. I thought we should, but the Countess refused and waited until her child's turn was routinely called.

On this visit I was very amused when after the lunch break I noticed that a few of the children had obviously fallen into the river.

"How did these children manage to fall into the river?" I asked.

"They were guddling fish," was the reply. To guddle, the children lay on the riverbank and caught fish with their bare hands.

When I entered my car for my journey home, two lovely fresh trout lay on the seat. I was very pleased but a little apprehensive as it was an offence to fish in the river which ran through the Earl's estate; the estate bailiffs had a habit of stopping vehicles in their search for poachers. Fortunately, my journey home was uneventful.

On my return journey to the school I asked the teacher if I could thank the pupil for the gift of the trout. She said, "You can try, but no one will admit to it." I did, but no one responded.

Then it was suggested that I should ask the class for those who guddled fish to stand up. When the question was put to them, the whole class stood up.

The next time I met the Countess was at a banquet. She was very pleasant company during the meal, and we recounted several amusing stories. One tale I told was about two British sailors who were on a visit to Sweden. On the Sunday they decided to attend church. Because of the language problem and their ignorance of the form of service, they decided to follow someone into the church and to watch what he or she would do during the service.

They picked on a distinguished-looking gentleman, followed him into the church and sat on the pew behind him. When he stood up, they stood up, and so on until toward the end the preacher made a special announcement and their distinguished gentleman stood up. So did the two sailors, to the obvious embarrassment of the congregation. Later they found that the preacher had announced a baptism and asked for the father to stand up.

The Countess was very amused at this and said, "In Sweden this could have happened when there is doubt about the father." Then she told me she had a Swedish heritage.

In another rural district the poor quality of the water produced interesting results. In a general discussion over coffee with the local doctors, a reference was made to "the Diarrhoea Season". On enquiry, I was told that every spring there was an outbreak in the town.

What could be the cause? Heavy spring rains? Run off? Water supply?

An inspection of the local water supply revealed that river water was channelled through a system of grids to a settling tank and chlorinated by a rather primitive method. This was probably adequate when the flow was leisurely, but with heavy spring run off the settling tank was inadequate and the chlorination plant did not respond to the copious increase in organic matter. Water tests produced high coliform counts, confirming the need for changes in the system.

CHAPTER 6

MORE HEALTH HAZARDS

Apart from the problems associated with water and sewage, communicable disease had a high priority, and the fresh country air did not produce immunity. In fact, the area was attractive to tourists, and food hygiene was an important responsibility.

One group reported an outbreak of food poisoning and, on enquiry, it was stated that they had eaten at a local "Two Star" hotel. Under the "star" system, these hotels must provide a high standard of cuisine and meals for non-residents.

The manageress welcomed me, but was disturbed by the suggestion that this group of customers had been indisposed following a visit to her dining-room. The hotel was well appointed with a high standard of comfort, but my visit to the kitchen was not so reassuring. So much so that I had my inspector carry out a detailed inspection, and laboratory samples were taken from members of the kitchen staff. We were too late for obtaining samples of the food served to the complainants.

Following the inspection, the hotel was served notice under the Food Hygiene Regulations 1955 to clean up and make structural changes. This produced an irate letter from the London headquarters with veiled threats of prosecution. My response was to detail the facts and continue my threats of closure.

A visit by two representatives from London followed. After more threats of court action, they were reminded that the situation was still not public, but if they persisted in their opposition, I would be bound to report publicly to my Council; that the Food Hygiene Regulations were very specific in their powers; and given these facts, any litigation would hardly be in the hotel's best interest. In the end, they agreed to carry out our recommendations.

The irony of this case was that the food poisoning eventually was found not to originate from this hotel. Our laboratory tests did not confirm the organism, and after more intensive questioning, the victims remembered they had made another stop on the way home. The source of the infection was traced to that cafe.

Still, I did not consider the action taken as a miscarriage of justice. The hotel's kitchen premises and practices were well below the standards set out in the regulations; it was only a matter of time before something would happen.

As a result of this exercise we proceeded to inspect all the premises affected by the new regulations; fortunately, there were only a few that were below standard, but those few certainly required drastic changes.

The role of an infection carrier is not always clear. For example, one case involved an elderly lady who had operated a pub and restaurant for years. She was a typhoid carrier, was very particular with her personal hygiene, and no outbreaks had previously been attributed to her.

During one of our regular coffee breaks, one of the doctors told me he was admitting for observation a patient with "pyrexia of unknown origin". The patient had had a prolonged fever, was constipated but had few clinical signs. I suggested that the patient should not be admitted until we had examined her again. As she was already on her way, we carried out our examination in the ambulance when it arrived. This revealed a slow pulse, some enlargement of the spleen and tell-tale rose spots on her skin. The diagnosis of typhoid fever was made, and she was sent to the fever hospital.

How did she get it? The patient's mother, the elderly lady referred to above, had suffered a very severe attack of diarrhoea with some incontinence, and her daughter and a neighbour had nursed her. The cause of the old lady's diarrhoea was not known at that time, however; there was no doubt about the daughter. In the middle of the investigation we found that the neighbour had been admitted to hospital with acute appendicitis. The surgeon was immediately informed that she had been nursing a possible typhoid patient. It was later confirmed that the neighbour had suffered a perforation of the bowel with acute peritonitis due to the typhoid bacillus.

We were able to trace the history of this infection back to the husband, who had been infected during the First World War. Soon after the war he had died, but infected his wife who had become a permanent carrier. This was confirmed when the old lady died some time later from an unrelated disease: at post mortem she was found to have typhoid cholecystitis, i.e., chronic inflammation of the gall-bladder, due to the typhoid bacillus.

Another infection to be feared at that time was Poliomyelitis, and we had a mild outbreak. One big healthy muscular man succumbed quickly to his attack. He was seen in morning surgery by his doctor, his complaint, low back pain. A few hours later he was seriously ill with difficulty in breathing. He was rushed to hospital, put in the iron lung, but died soon after.

Shortly following this outbreak the Salk vaccine became available in limited quantities. We started vaccinating school children. At the local convent school we vaccinated all the girls, and afterward I had some spare vaccine. The Mother

Superior was a very pleasant and attractive lady, and I had
visited her school on a number of occasions. I suggested to her
that we should vaccinate the staff. When she agreed, I decided
to play a practical joke on her. While the nurse and I prepared
the vaccine for injection, the Mother Superior pulled up her
sleeve to expose her shoulder.

"No, Sister, the children have the injection into the shoulder, adults must have it in the gluteus maximus, in other words,
the buttocks." Her embarrassment increased with the exposure of skin until we could not contain our laughter; then she
had the injection into the shoulder. Luckily for us she appreciated the joke.

Hazards are not always due to infections. This time the peril
and consequential discomfort were of my own making. We
had spent a very pleasant summer afternoon on the beach
with our daughter and her friends. They had had a lot of fun
in a kayak, and when they tired of it, I decided to take a turn. I
did not have a swimsuit, so dressed in my jacket, shirt with
collar and tie, socks and shoes, I was pushed out on to the
water. After paddling around for a bit, I decided to torment
the children by using the paddle to splash water on them, and
then, before they could catch me, paddle off into deeper water.
When this amusement was over I resumed leisurely paddling,
and was quite oblivious to the manoeuvres of my daughter
and her friends as they sneaked up behind and eventually
tipped the kayak over. I was not an expert in getting out of an
upturned kayak in the gentle sea waves, but after several attempts made it to the surface, amidst the laughter and cheers
of the children. My journey back home was soggy, but my
feelings were assuaged by the happy laughter of the children
at my predicament.

About this time we were blessed by another launching – the
birth of our son, Iain. I had a wager on the result of the birth
with my daughter, and I had guessed rightly the sex of the
baby. When she was informed, there was silence for a few

minutes, then she said, "You'll be pleased, you'll now be able to get an electric train set!" I had tried hard to get her interested in such a pastime.

While trains keep to the rails, our son was not so easily confined. He had a knack for manipulating anything mechanical or gadgetry. No matter how we tried to secure the gate and the confines of our property, he found a way out. It was not unusual for him to get out with his walker and to be returned in the arms of our neighbour, who was a policeman.

Problems with security are one thing, but poor housing conditions could be a major problem. Housing was an important function of the Medical Office of Health. Under the Housing Act 1957, it was the duty of the local authority to inspect their district to ascertain whether any dwelling house was unfit for habitation. If it could be made fit at a reasonable expense, a notice was served on the owner. If not, a demolition order was required.

When the M.O.H. made an official representation to the local authority that dwelling houses in an area were unfit for human habitation, or were by reason of their bad arrangement, or the narrowness or bad arrangement of the streets, dangerous or injurious to the health of the inhabitants of the area, it could be declared "a clearance area". When this happened, the owner was ordered to demolish the buildings in the area, or the local authority could purchase the land and themselves secure the demolition of the buildings.

In one case the representation for a clearance area proved to be confusing to say the least. The owner happened to be the Chairman of the Council. To add to our difficulties the lawyer for the Chairman was also the part-time Clerk of the Council. As you would expect, especially in a small urban area, the representation to Council proved to be a very stormy process, but finally the authority passed the resolution.

However, my problems were not over. Objectors had to be given a hearing before a person appointed by the Minister of the National Government. Normally the Council's position would be led by the Clerk, but he was speaking for the objector. Thus I had to present the Council's position and the details of my representation. The press had a field day. The Council's resolution was upheld and, in spite of the bitterness of the attacks and after the process was completed, the Clerk, the Chairman and I finished up in the local bar, and there were no recriminations.

Soon after this episode I was trapped in a different situation. A gentleman was shown into my office, told me he represented Industrial Insurance Companies and that his companies proposed a banquet to publicise their business. Would I attend? How could one refuse the offer of a free meal!

Once I had accepted the bait, I was hooked. The request was made for me to be the keynote speaker. "How can I speak on a subject which is practically unknown to me?" With smooth persuasive words I was assured that the necessary information would be provided, that the speech should be amusing as well as informative, and that most of the men attending would be known to me: I could tell a few jokes to the "boys". No mention was made of ladies; my wife wasn't even invited.

Armed with my speech, which included a few stories that could hardly be repeated in the company of ladies, I was struck with consternation when I entered the foyer of the White Swan Hotel to find a number of prominent men accompanied by their ladies, all moving in the direction of the banqueting hall.

The meal was sumptuous, but instead of gastric gratification, cerebration had priority while I altered my speech. To increase my distress, the chairman had over-indulged in food and wine, and fell asleep just before he was due to make the introductions. In spite of all these set-backs my speech was apparently a success.

Another banquet was much more enjoyable, but the outing almost ended in injury. We were thrilled to receive an invitation to be the guests of the medical fraternity at their dinner and dance in Bishop Auckland. We set off on the Friday and arrived for lunch at the home of Nancy and Bill Steele, our friends from Coundon. It was close to Christmas, and we were foolish enough to promise the children we would take them the next day to Darlington for a visit with Santa Claus.

The evening was most enjoyable and we returned with Bill and Nancy about 1 a.m. The coffee-pot was put on, and we sat for another two hours reminiscing. The children were very excited, and we were roused by them around 7 a.m. After a hearty breakfast we set off for Darlington, returning for a heavy lunch.

About 4:30 p.m. we set off for home; it was dark, it was raining, the heater was on, my wife and daughter were sleeping, and I had difficulty in keeping my eyes open. Normally I would pull over to the side and shut my eyes for a few minutes, but as we were approaching the outskirts of Gateshead I knew the sleepiness would leave me when we left the highway and had the town lights. I lowered my car window to let the cold air play on my face and reduced speed as we approached a roundabout. One minute the road sign for Gateshead was visible, the next minute I was awakened by a bump as we mounted the roundabout and the road sign was approaching fast. Fortunately, I had time to swerve and miss the sign.

After five years in the post I was beginning to get restless. My staff was very competent, services were operating smoothly, and I did not feel challenged. Moreover, with the birth of our son, we needed a bigger home, and a safer one.

At first we started looking for a building site, and soon found one in Lesbury village. Before proceeding with the purchase, we spent some time deciding the plan of the house which would suit our needs and the location. Subsequently, we arrived at the estate office to discover that the site had been sold twenty-four hours before. As we watched developments, we saw the house we had planned materialise before our eyes. In spite of this we became very good friends of the owners, and still occasionally visit them in the same house.

Should I look for a new position, or should we continue our search for a new home? To our surprise both opportunities presented themselves at approximately the same time. We decided success would determine our direction.

The house in question was owned by a member of the Hardy family, a name well known internationally for its manufacture and sale of fishing equipment. I had lived in it for a short time when it was a guest house. Often I had thought it would be wonderful to own it.

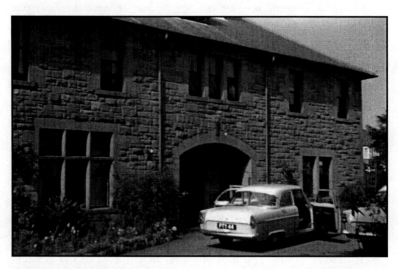

"THE CLOSE", ANLWICK

Built in 1911, the house was constructed in sandstone, and stood on just over half an acre of ground. The rooms were all very spacious, with a most attractive lounge. It had a beautiful granite fireplace, and windows that reached from floor to ceiling. There was a library, conservatory, dining-room, kitchen and tiled laundry-room, all on the ground floor. A beautiful stairway led up from a spacious hall to the three bedrooms, and in the attic there were another three bedrooms.

About this time Mr. Hardy died, and a week following his funeral my secretary told me that his widow was selling the house. She suggested I should phone Mrs. Hardy, but I refused because of the funeral being so recent. However, like all good secretaries, she paid no attention, and soon Mrs. Hardy was on the telephone inviting me down for tea. Thus we became the proud owners of "The Close" in Alnwick.

Just prior to this development a Senior Medical Officer's position in Edinburgh was advertised in the British Medical Journal. To me it was very appealing, as the challenge was the development of community services proposed under the new Mental Health (Scotland) Act 1960, as well as community services for the disabled. There would be no increase in salary.

I was not very optimistic about success in the application; weeks passed without a response, and as we became involved in moving to our new residence, I put the job out of my mind.

We had been settled in our new home about three months, when out of the blue a letter arrived inviting me to Edinburgh for an interview. Oh dear! What should I do?

Still feeling pessimistic about the possibility of attaining the post, but curious and interested, I decided to accept the invitation. My pessimism was not relieved when I first appeared outside the Public Heath Department in Johnston Terrace one sunny morning. I was faced by a grim and dirty-looking building, which appeared to be misnamed. On the other side of the street the menacing grey rock rose steeply to end in the ramparts of the castle, and cast its shadow. This was followed by the inevitable wait in an ante-chamber, which was also gloomy, and there were many candidates.

The interview was very pleasant, and to my surprise I was asked to wait. The surprise was even greater when I was asked to return to the interview room, and the position was offered to me. Normally one is sent home and later a letter is received indicating success or failure. In this case there was no opportunity to discuss the offer with my wife. The decision had to be made immediately. I accepted.

We were extremely sorry to leave North Northumberland and to leave our dream home, but I realised that from the long-term point of view, I was too young to remain in a position which was becoming a dull routine.

CHAPTER 7

THE TEAMS

Needless to say, my wife was not too happy at the prospect of leaving our new home so soon, nor did we relish the thought of starting over again to make new friends and to leave the many good friends we had made. Further, the very friendly and social cohesion one experiences in a country town would be lost.

While the social atmosphere was more than likely to change, the opportunities for academic and professional advancement and collaboration in Edinburgh were outstanding. Starting as a Senior Medical Officer of Health, and soon after as Deputy Medical Officer, ten very challenging and rewarding years were spent from 1960 to 1970.

At times it was difficult to conceive that my employer was the City of Edinburgh. I was indeed fortunate to have a Health Authority that allowed me full scope in my endeavour to establish effective services in the community for the mentally disordered and the physically handicapped. Restrictions were never wilfully employed by the various committees with which I had been involved: they were always interested and sympathetic to the claims of the disabled.

The aim of the Mental Health (Scotland) Act of 1960 was to

ensure that, whenever possible, the mentally disordered patient could have the same ready access, without formality, to
care and treatment as the patient suffering from a physical
disorder. It also provided special safeguards to protect patients being treated under compulsory detention.

The term "mental disorder" was used to cover all forms of
mental ill health, and it included mental handicap. Application for compulsory admission to hospital or guardianship of
the Local Health Authority had to be made by a relative or a
Mental Health Officer (M.H.O.) of the Local Health Authority,
with the support of two medical recommendations; and in
Scotland it had to be approved by the Sheriff.

Emergency recommendations required a certificate from a
medical practitioner who had personally examined the patient
with the consent of a relative or M.H.O.

The need to integrate Mental Health Services was recognised
by both clinicians and administrators, and when a large city
like Edinburgh was served by three mental hospitals and a
large hospital for the mentally handicapped, the potential problems under the new Act were viewed with concern. Moreover,
other services, such as the general hospital, geriatric, general
medical and voluntary services, all required participation and
co-operation in the overall scheme.

Preparation for the inauguration of the 1960 Act prompted
the need for a survey of the existing Mental Health Services.
At the instigation of Dr. H. Seiler, the Medical Officer of Health,
the Edinburgh Corporation, the South-East Scotland Regional
Hospital Board and the Edinburgh Executive Council (for general practitioners) appointed a working party to undertake a
survey and report.

The working party consisted of psychiatrists from the mental hospitals serving the city, medical representatives of the
Regional Hospital Board with their psychiatric advisor, the
senior medical assistant for the Mental Health Services of the
city, and three general medical practitioners. The working party

was chaired by Dr. H. Seiler.

Following their report, in December 1959, the three statutory bodies invited the working party to continue as a Medical Co-ordinating Advisory Committee to advise on the development of a unified mental health service, research, and the education of the public on mental health matters.

Soon after this I joined the advisory committee and later became a member of the Board of Management for the Royal Edinburgh Hospital, which was the major mental hospital serving the city. I was also privileged to join the medical staff as an honorary clinical assistant.

Before going to Edinburgh, my experience and knowledge of psychiatrists and psychiatric medicine was extremely limited. In my ignorance, I was more apprehensive then of the motives of psychiatrists. Perhaps I felt that my thoughts, actions and emotions would be controlled by them. The psychiatrists even have a name for these feelings, "passivity feelings". Needless to say, I found no ulterior motives and was extremely grateful for the way in which I was readily accepted as a member of the psychiatric team as well as being part of the administration.

It was necessary therefore to embark on a training programme. My mentor was Dr. Jim Affleck, Physician Superintendent and Psychiatric Consultant, a most competent teacher and friend from whose teachings and advice I have benefited greatly.

The University Department of Psychiatry also provided me with invaluable training, and when the department moved to new premises at the Royal Edinburgh Hospital, it was possible to participate in seminars and other postgraduate training programmes.

To facilitate better communication with the voluntary associations, it was necessary to become involved with the Scottish Association for Mental Health. I joined as a Member of Council and later became Chairman of the Executive Committee.

Close working relationships were developed with the Scottish Society for Mentally Handicapped Children and the Edinburgh Committee for the Co-ordination of Services for the Disabled. Certainly, with these multiple interests and considerations there was a substantial demand on my time, although sometimes it was possible to mix work with pleasure. For example, during the winter months senior medical, nursing and administrative staff met with their spouses on a regular basis, and at our own expense, at the George Hotel in Edinburgh for supper and dancing.

We were also fortunate to have good neighbours. One of our neighbours was manager of a large department store called "Patrick Thomson's". We attended with Tom and Chrissie Hunter many functions organised by the staff; formal dress for senior staff activities and more relaxed attire and distractions for other levels – all very enjoyable. On two occasions we were privileged to attend a garden party at Holyrood Palace.

At the same time, our son continued his wanderlust. Our home was located in a new housing development, and it took some time for us to provide fencing. He was also very interested in the construction activities around us, and at times my wife was distraught by his straying. His interest in construction and engineering should have forewarned us about his future career.

In spite of his interest in all things mechanical, on one occasion at least he proved to be a good diagnostician and caused me some embarrassment. My daughter had complained of feeling unwell and of pain and stiffness on one side of her jaw. With the customary parental assertiveness I assumed she was reluctant to go to school and gave her the usual response. Later our son had the same complaint, and when he was admonished he responded with the question, "Dad, don't you think I have the mumps?" His diagnosis was correct. Our daughter, consequently, was not impressed by the cursory treatment she had received from me, and blamed the outbreak of mumps in the school on her neglectful and unsympathetic father, who incidentally worked for public health.

Another upset occurred on one of the few occasions when I was baby-sitting. I loaded the dishwasher and being unable to find the regular detergent, mistakenly assumed that any other detergent would do, with the inevitable result. When the machine started making peculiar noises, I found the kitchen full of soapsuds and was faced with the daunting task of removing the evidence.

So much for my personal rashness. As previously stated, the city was served by three mental hospitals and a hospital for the mentally handicapped. The Royal Edinburgh Hospital was situated in Morningside, relatively close to the centre of the city. It was opened in 1813 and has an interesting history. The founder was Dr. Andrew Duncan, who was influenced by the death of Robert Ferguson in the most miserable conditions, which prevailed in Edinburgh's Bedlam. Robert Ferguson was a Scottish poet who influenced and inspired Robert Burns; Dr. Duncan had been his medical attendant.

In 1965 a new clinic (the Andrew Duncan Clinic) with 100 beds and a Professorial Clinical Unit of 60 beds, combined with a day hospital for 45 patients, was opened by the Queen Mother.

We were privileged to have lunch with the Queen Mother. During the meal she asked if we still had the waitress who had served all the members of the Royal Family at one time or another when they were in Scotland. If so, could she see her?

Contained within the grounds of the hospital was the Scottish School of Hospital Catering, where the "waitress" Peggy worked and had helped on numerous occasions at banquets for members of the Royal Family. I was able to find Peggy, and she and the Queen Mother had a long conversation. Peggy was also able to produce the silver tray she had received with the inscribed signatures of the Royal Family. The Queen Mother was charming and quickly set us at ease; Peggy had a fond memory, which she will always cherish.

The old part of the Royal Edinburgh Hospital had some attractive and historical buildings. The Grand Hall at Craig House was the setting for a banquet one year for a group attending an Anglo-American Psychiatric Convention. The hall had a gallery and numerous oil-paintings and stuffed animal heads at intervals around the walls. It was approached by a wonderful marble stairway. A group of us were standing with our drinks, talking to some psychiatrists from Texas. We were interrupted several times by a little man who complained to us that "things are floating down from the roof". We looked around, saw nothing to confirm his statement, and wondered if our little psychiatrist had developed some of his patients' symptoms. Later, as one of the Texan psychiatrists was emphasising a point and stuck out his hand containing his glass, there was a plop, and something landed in his drink. Then we noticed that an uninvited bird had gained entrance and when it flew from one perch to another it disturbed the dust, and things did float down from the roof, as did his excreta, much to the embarrassment of the hosts.

The new additions brought a reorganisation of responsibility and an increased variety of treatment options for the hospital. The Nurse Training School arranged to take student nurses from the general hospitals for eight weeks of psychiatric experience; nursing students from Edinburgh University Nursing Studies Unit were given twelve weeks of experience, and arrangements were made for a programme of research in psychiatric nursing. In-service training for health visitors was also provided.

The Occupational Therapy Department was expanded, and there was also an expansion of the rehabilitation programme; in some cases the ward was used as a hostel so that the patient could return to work while still remaining under hospital care.

Case conferences continued on a multi-disciplinary basis; they included health visitors, mental health offices, and the disablement resettlement officers (D.R.O.s) from the Ministry of Labour Rehabilitation Unit. Relationships among the various professions involved were excellent, and continuity of care was ensured by the attendance of the local health authority staff. In addition, the follow-up by the latter allowed for case conference review when problems arose with psychiatric patients within the community. Similar case conferences and reviews occurred at the other hospitals.

Getting different professional workers together doesn't automatically ensure a proficient team. Sometimes the team members are not always aware of their own limitations or of the role of others in the team. One dictionary defines "Team Work" as "two or more oxen, horses, dogs, etc, harnessed to draw together. If the amount of effort is not equal, or the pull is in different directions, then the team is quickly disorganised and becomes ineffective". Another definition is "work done by organised division of labour with regard to the success of the whole, rather than personal exploits".

For the Mental Health Services to be effective and efficient, therefore, respect and trust must be earned by all the members, and a rapid response to the concerns and needs of patients is paramount. Frustration in hospital or community care should be recognised and dealt with expeditiously; this requires a clear line of command and responsibility.

In the hospital, the treatment team should be responsible for the day to day treatment and supervision, and there must be a smooth and informed transfer of the patient to community care if these services are required. In our case, if problems couldn't be resolved within the team, the physician superintendent became involved, or the physician in charge of the Community Services intervened.

When disputes arose between a hospital and local authority services and could not be settled, the issue was referred to the Medical Co-ordinating Advisory Committee.

To ensure that the professions were informed, and clearly

understood their responsibilities and the range of services open to them, a number of steps were taken by the Advisory Committee, including advice on the development of new services.

First, a handbook on facilities for the care of the mentally disordered, chronic sick and aged was published in 1961. It included information on the arrangements, under the Mental Health (Scotland) Act 1960, for hospital care, after-care and guardianships. Telephone numbers were given and every attempt was made to answer the queries likely to be raised by family doctors and other professionals. This proved to be a very popular resource.

Several symposia were held to inform general practitioners about the changes under the new Act, and a limited number of clinical assistantships in psychiatry as well as teaching sessions on mental handicapped, pediatric and adult psychiatry were provided.

The 1960 Act led to the transfer of mental health functions and responsibilities from the Social Welfare Department to the Health Department, and as part of the reorganization and the Act, five M.H.O.s were appointed. They were based at the department's main office and were on a 24-hour rotation for emergencies, sharing in appointments to the hospitals.

Qualified social workers were in short supply; consequently the decision was made to recruit psychiatric nurses and/or social workers. It was also agreed that if a psychiatric nurse was appointed, he or she should, at a later date, be encouraged to take Social Work training.

Plans were made in conjunction with the staff of the Department of Psychological Medicine for a short orientation course. The object of the course was to give the M.H.O.s a general review of the Mental Health Services, clinical psychiatry interpersonal relationships, the problems of rehabilitation, and the working of the new Act. Officers from other local authorities were invited. Thirty-five Welfare and M.H.O.s from 27 authorities throughout Scotland attended from 26th March to

13th April 1962. The course was very successful and popular, and was repeated annually, sometimes as a refresher or as a full course, depending on the demand.

In the spring of 1961 the Medical Co-ordinating Advisory Committee was approached by the University of Edinburgh Settlement with an offer of facilities for work in the mental health field. The premises could be used for separate group activities, a gymnasium providing space for games, a theatre, and space for dancing.

A club was started in the building as part of a rehabilitation regime for selected in-patients of the two principal hospitals serving the city. Later an Evening Club was started for ex-patients.

In planning our first hostel for the mentally ill we required a number of answers. For these we went to the advisory committee and to other local authorities who had experience in providing hostels.

A hotel was purchased in Northumberland Street, near the centre of Edinburgh. It was of Georgian architecture, built in the early 1800s with two storeys plus a basement. It accommodated 25 patients, plus the warden and his wife.

At the time, it was ascertained that the people who gained most from a hostel were the long-stay schizophrenics, who had no home or interested relatives. For this kind of patient, it was decided that the warden should be an experienced mental health nurse in order to be able to deal with any disturbed behaviour of some of the residents, and to ensure continuation of drug therapy.

There is no doubt that the advisory committee provided a strong influence when budget or planning submissions were made to the city, and it facilitated co-operation between institutions and staff. It was also recognised that there was a need for social work input, and accordingly the Professor of Social Administration joined the advisory committee.

CHAPTER 8

"TEACH ME TO FEEL ANOTHER'S WOE"

Invariably a number of mentally disordered patients are arrested by the police because of their conduct, and subsequently face court appearances and detention in prison cells. While a few require punishment for their crimes, a good proportion are in need of help, and imprisonment only aggravates their condition. Moreover, there is frequently a need to act quickly in case compulsory emergency admission to hospital may be required.

The police approached our department for help. We agreed that when a person was arrested and was obviously mentally ill, or had a history of mental disorder, then we would be notified. We would then consult with the family doctor, consultant psychiatrist, or both. If there was no family doctor or the patient was unable to give details, or the case was urgent, the mental health officer and I or my assistant would be called to examine the patient in the cells and arrange immediate hospital treatment, when deemed necessary.

In other cases, after making enquiries, we would give the Public Prosecutor our views on the patient's condition, and advise whether he could be confined in prison without detriment to his health, or whether a psychiatric report should be requested. Sometimes, it was necessary to appear in court to give these opinions.

These arrangements proved helpful to the police, and it determined quicker and better disposal of these cases.

One other problem raised by the police was the care of prisoners threatening suicide, sometimes because of social problems. In these cases an M.H.O. would be called with back-up from a psychiatrist or from us, if required.

Weekends appeared to be busy times for the police, and for us Monday morning reviews were not uncommon. In fact, it was sometimes very difficult to obtain a history, etc., because of the noise from the cells, which were frequently overcrowded.

Of course, early morning calls were quite frequent. One morning around 3 a.m., I was called to the central police station. On entering, I was met by a most disconsolate police sergeant.

"What's wrong, Sergeant, you look miserable?"

"Thank goodness you're here, Doc. Take your pick. We have the Pope in one cell and Jesus Christ in the other, and they are both causing an uproar."

The man claiming to be the Pope had upset mass in the Cathedral and was clearly psychotic. In fact, it took us some time to find his real identity. He was removed to hospital on an emergency treatment order.

The other one purporting to be Jesus Christ had upset the guards at Edinburgh Castle by demanding entry and attempting to preach a sermon to them. The guards had been very patient; they didn't think much of his sermon, and when he attempted to force an entry, they sent for the police. After about ten minutes of questioning, I decided he was not mentally ill and said:

"What are you wanting? You are not mentally ill, although it's obvious you are trying to convince me you are suffering from schizophrenia."

After some more bizarre behaviour, the man admitted that

every winter he put on this act so that he could have accommodation and food in hospital. Some weeks later I met the same gentleman in another mental hospital when attending a Psychiatric Association meeting. He sidled up to me and pleaded that I would not tell. I didn't tell.

Another troublesome case was a lady who suffered from manic-depressive psychosis. Whenever she had a manic outburst she would strip off her clothes and run about in public. One day when I was called, she was found partially clothed in a cell, elated and walking back and forth. The police decided that she could not be controlled in an ambulance, and would take her in one of their vehicles. In spite of my objections and warning not to manhandle her, a policewoman and two burly policemen grabbed her. She struggled and threatened to "piss on them!" When they ignored her obvious protests and threats, she arched her body and urinated on the policewoman who was holding her legs. She was quickly dropped; recognising me, she took my arm and we walked gracefully to the police van.

All the cases were not seen in the police cells. One foreign tourist to the city was preventing guests from entering or leaving his hotel. He was big and powerful, so menacing that the police were reluctant to tackle him.

When persuasion failed they sent for help. My rather petite female mental health officer and I arrived to find two policemen and a throng of onlookers. We went up to the man, my mental health officer spoke quietly to him, he took her arm and we proceeded calmly to my car and to the hospital.

Another case was more dramatic, and for the only time in my professional career did I feel my life was threatened. An American tourist, a man in his late thirties, had been arrested for failing to pay his rail fare and was taken to the U.S. Consulate. His odd behaviour resulted in a call to our department. My mental health officer and I were shown into the Consul's office; the Consul was seated at his desk, a secretary and security man were also present, and a very agitated man was moving around the room.

It was soon obvious that the man suffered from paranoid schizophrenia with delusions about the F.B.I. and the Russian K.G.B. As he became more disturbed and concerned about "spies" he suddenly reached into his pocket and produced a loaded revolver. The other occupants rushed from the room, leaving my M.H.O. and me facing the gunman. Fortunately the man did not pull the trigger when the exodus occurred. The gun was pointed at me as we continued our discussion about the spies and the K.G.B. Knowing that any attempt to take the gun from him would probably end with someone being shot, I continued to talk, gradually directing the conversation to the gun and its make until, with great relief on our part, he handed the gun to me so that I could inspect it.

Continuing to talk about his fears and his delusions, we finally persuaded him to come with us in our car.

Then there was Mabel, the prostitute. She was a big powerful girl, who suffered from rather explosive outbursts when she attacked property or persons. These incidents were followed by arrest and court appearances. Tired of these repeated arrests, futile remedies, masses of paperwork, etc. the police appealed for some help. Not an easy task.

When she was age fourteen her mother had died and her father, who was an alcoholic, threw her out of the house into the streets where prostitution was a common solution for survival. Any attempt to change this occupation is fraught with enormous difficulties, the principal ones being the alternative job opportunities and the related drop in income.

On the positive side, Mabel wanted to leave her profession and to control her offensive behaviour. Many attempts were made to find her other employment, only to fail when she became disillusioned by the poor monetary recompense, or following an outburst, which resulted in her being fired, or she just walked off the job. Yet we persisted.

To help reduce or prevent her sudden and violent behaviour, we arranged that when she began to feel stressed or very angry, she would walk away from the provocation and telephone one of my staff or me; she was given several phone numbers. This arrangement worked quite well, but it also created some embarrassing situations.

It was not unusual for me to be interrupted at a meeting and informed that "Your prostitute friend is in urgent need to speak to you on the phone, and she has vehemently spurned any form of refusal!"

One Sunday evening she phoned me at home, very agitated and confused. After about ten minutes or so she settled down, and I suggested that she should go to her sister's home. Her response was a reiteration of the reasons her sister would not accept her, but she ended by stating her sister might accept her if I took her there. Finally, and rather reluctantly, I agreed. As I drove towards the centre of the city, I suddenly realised that I had agreed to pick up a well-known prostitute, in the red-light district, close to a bus stop, which was a popular rendezvous for some of our clients. Fortunately this episode ended without further incident.

As time passed, and she managed to remain employed in a legitimate business without the usual upsets, we began to congratulate ourselves that we had been successful in our approach. Our ego was soon punctured when she decided to visit her old haunts, succumbed to the temptation to earn some extra money at her old trade, and returned to her hostel and ripped it apart.

I received an urgent call from the hostel, and when I got there the proprietor, the volunteers and all the residents had locked themselves in their rooms while Mabel continued to rampage. She recognised me, fortunately stopped her destruction, and sat down on the remains of a chair.

After some sobbing, she blurted out that after the man had paid her for her services, she felt for the first time a feeling of deep remorse, which she could not accept or control. The owner of the hostel was one of the most saintly persons I have ever known, and Mabel was soon accepted back into the family.

The hostel was situated in the centre of the city and the owner, a devout Catholic lady, had purchased it and operated it with the aid of a priest and volunteers. It was a refuge for abused women, prostitutes, and indeed for any woman who needed a refuge. Her only condition was that residents should not continue in prostitution while living there.

Following this episode, Mabel continued to work, and after several months we were beginning to feel comfortable again with our efforts. Regrettably, the next incident proved to be more serious, removing her from our care.

Mabel had been baby-sitting for her sister, and the constant crying of the baby had become so intolerable that she put a pillow over the baby's face and killed the child. When seen later in prison, Mabel was quite remorseful and realistic. Shortly afterwards I left for Canada, and hoped that she managed to overcome her problems and maintain the life she tried so hard to achieve.

I also met quite a number of elderly people, some in very pleasant circumstances, and others in extremely unhappy and pathetic conditions. When an elderly person is able-bodied and mentally fit, he or she normally does not require help, nor do they welcome interference.

But problems usually arise as soon as self-care has broken down and there are no relatives or friends; or even when there is support, the infirmity of an aged person may prove an excessive burden on the family or neighbours.

Sometimes, especially after bereavement, the surviving spouse cannot accept the tragic event and, in one case I experienced, the husband continued his normal routine of taking breakfast to the bedroom, and in every way pretending that his wife was still alive. Moreover, in this situation, the survivor has to withdraw from society because it will question the facade.

On occasions one sees an elderly person dwelling in a state of extreme squalor, and in these cases the home is utterly filthy. Thick layers of dust coat every object, tattered remains of curtains droop at the windows, which are dark and unwashed, and underfoot one tramples on mouldering food and rubbish, sometimes even excreta. Half-empty tins, used dishes and decaying food can be seen in the kitchen and elsewhere, and there are usually stacks of old newspapers. Somewhere on a bed, or in a dirty chair, we find a gaunt person with grimy clothes and unwashed skin. Their disposition is often hostile.

A number of these persons are very unwilling to relinquish their slim hold on independence, and refuse all offers of help. In such conditions, a compulsory removal had to be considered. Under Section 47 of the National Assistance Act 1948, the local health authority had power to act.

The Act stated that "for the purpose of securing necessary care and attention, persons could be removed to suitable premises in circumstances where they (a) were suffering from grave chronic disease or being aged, infirm or physically incapacitated, were living in unsanitary conditions, and (b) were unable to devote to themselves and were not receiving from other persons, proper care and attention."

The Medical Officer of Health had to certify in writing the need for this action to his local authority and, in turn, the local authority had to apply to the courts for an order to remove the person. The order could then authorise detention for any period not exceeding three months, but further application could be made to extend this period when deemed necessary. In urgent cases, a simplified form was used, and the Medical Officer of Health could apply directly to the court.

This section of the Act was only used when all else failed; in fact, it was very distressing to everyone, including the enforcers, to witness an elderly person being carried by policemen, screaming and kicking, to an ambulance.

Attempts to help, without compulsion, were usually made over a period of months, and in some cases over a year or more.

One such elderly person was reported to us by a neighbour, who had supplied a meal regularly to this lady, but who resented the empty wine bottles which littered the house, and the fact that the person she was trying to help thanked her with abusive language. In addition, while this elderly lady was able to carry the full bottles upstairs to her apartment, she was apparently incapable of carrying the empties down again.

After suffering this situation for a prolonged period and observing a serious deterioration in the situation, the neighbour withdrew her services and asked for our help.

A number of calls were made to the home, but she refused to open the door and shouted abuse at us. We became more concerned when we found that her trips to the pub for cheap wine had ceased, and her neighbours did not know if she was getting any food.

A court order was obtained; when we entered the house we had to walk along a passageway lined about three to four feet high on either side by empty wine bottles, and the bedroom also had an accumulation of empty bottles. The house was filthy, and we could only find some scraps of edible food. There were some bits of putrid food and some curdled milk. The lady had suffered a mild cerebral thrombosis, and we admitted her to hospital.

From her house we removed 2700 empty wine bottles, 250 empty and unwashed milk bottles, and 29 bags of rubbish weighing over two tons. While she was in hospital we were able to obtain the services of university students, who cleaned up the home and decorated it as well. Our lady made a good recovery, and when she returned home arrangements were made for volunteers to visit her on a regular basis; the last I heard of her was that instead of imbibing cheap wine, she was having a more rewarding time entertaining her friends with tea and biscuits.

Another of these cases involved an elderly spinster who had worked in a bank until she retired. When her parents died she employed a housekeeper, but eventually got rid of the house-keeper and gradually shut herself off from the outside world. An electrician, who gained access to the house in order to read the meter and do some repairs, reported that the conditions were so appalling that "he could not eat any food afterwards for several days." Near the electric fire were large bundles of newspapers; there was a great deal of decomposing food lying about, her clothes were matted with food residue, and her legs covered with filthy bandages. She had burns on both legs from the electric fire, and a lot of unpleasant smell emanated from the sores.

Starting as a probable Section 47, the next case ended with amusing but touching effect. It concerned a lady in her early seventies. The owner of the apartment complained about the filth of the premises, and the abuse he received when collect-ing the rent. On my first visit, she wouldn't open the door but berated me with all kinds of threats and curses. On the second visit the door was partially opened and faeces thrown. More visits ultimately produced some semblance of normal behaviour and conversation; eventually I was invited inside to drink tea from a rather grimy cup. The interior had the usual signs of neglect and filth, and she appeared undernourished but otherwise healthy. We had some more tea breaks and dis-cussions about her plight before she agreed to move into a home. She agreed on the condition that I would take her and ensure that she would settle in.

On the day she moved I helped load her suitcase into the boot or trunk of my car, but she steadfastly refused to release a small bag which she firmly gripped. As we drove along I asked her why she was so protective of her bag. She said, "First tell me, will my room be reserved for me as long as I live, even if I go on vacation?"

"Yes, unless you take ill and require constant nursing care. But why do you ask?"

"Well, you got me thinking after our talk, I have a few relatives and fewer friends, not one of them has visited me or offered any help; in fact I've felt rejected and very lonely, life wasn't worth living. Yet they all know I have money, and when I die they will all appear like vultures, waiting to feed on my gold. So I decided to take my money out of the bank and to spend it on travel. All my worldly possessions are in my bag."

"Can I ask how much money you have?"

"Over thirty thousand pounds."

When I visited her about a week after her admission, she had befriended another old lady who had few financial resources. Soon after this I was asked to call and to give my opinion and advice on the trips they were planning. Their first trip was to London, but subsequently I received postcards from all over the world. Occasionally I was invited to the home to receive a summary of their exploits and to view their photographs. They were like two happy teenagers.

Several years elapsed while they continued their adventures, but it had to end. She sent for me when on her deathbed; as I entered the room she grinned when she saw me, and said, "I did it; I have spent every penny and had a great time. Now for the reckoning. You will find all my relatives and so-called friends knocking on your door, concerned about their inheritance. When they find there is nothing they will blame you for encouraging me to spend it. You can assure them I was of sound mind and knew exactly what I was doing." She then went on to thank me for helping her to come to her senses, and for helping to make her latter years so pleasant.

As expected, the relatives were very irate but not apologetic for their previous lack of interest.

In cases where the M.H.O. had reason to believe a person was mentally ill, living alone and not receiving care, and where he or she was refused admission, application could be made to the courts for a warrant to enter by force if necessary, and remove the patient to a place of safety. Application of this section of the Act could sometimes be very difficult, as usually the case was reported by neighbours; when investigated it was frequently found that you were becoming involved in a "cold war" between patient and neighbour, and at times it was difficult to distinguish genuine mental symptoms from battle cries.

One of the early cases under the Act, where there was some doubt about the state of mind, was a lady known to the department. Complaints were received that she was hammering on the walls, shouting and keeping the neighbours awake at nights. A number of calls were made to her home, but on each occasion Miss X refused to open the door, although it was known she was at home. The windows were dirty and covered with remnants of curtains and newspapers.

Her family doctor intervened and persuaded her to come to the department. It was obvious following her visits that she was eccentric, but it was felt that no compulsory action could be taken. Attempts were made to improve relationships, but these were only partly successful. Later she became more disturbed; the banging on the walls increased as well as the shouted abuse. After further consultation with her doctor and the neighbours, it was decided to apply for a warrant, and entry was obtained by the use of force.

The interior of the house was much worse than had been expected; the rooms were piled waist-high with an assortment of dirty clothes and rubbish collected from the street. She remained for several months under compulsory detention, but was eventually able to move to a nursing home.

Another group of people who feel rejected and lonely are the homeless of all ages, a group which society generally regards with disdain, and consequently we become insensitive to their needs. I was abruptly reminded of this when participating in a TV documentary. With the television camera crew we joined a line up one night awaiting admission to one of the city's winter shelters. It was about midnight, and as the cameras rolled I overheard two men at the head of the line complain that it was degrading to be "on camera" in such a condition. When we entered the hall I announced to the group the reason for the documentary, namely "the plight of the homeless", and also asked those who did not want to appear on camera to stand at one end of the hall and they would not be seen in the programme. Almost half of them made their wishes clear. If the remarks of the two men had not been heard, we would have probably continued shooting without giving them an option, or realising their sense of despair.

CHAPTER 9

"HANDICAPPED BUT HAPPY"

The title of this chapter was used by the Scottish Society for Mentally Handicapped Children for a film showing some aspects of the care of the mentally handicapped. To create this ideal is a formidable task, requiring the help and co-operation of a number of professional workers, the families, and the public in general.

As Medical Adviser to the Society, I had a lot of contact with the parents, and they were never hesitant in keeping me informed of their problems and of shortcomings within the service. At the same time, we shared in the planning and objectives of the service.

The birth of a baby is normally a happy event; for the midwife or doctor it usually gives tremendous satisfaction to see a happy mother and a healthy bouncing infant, a feeling of a job well done. There is great relief when the mother and the nurse or doctor find that the baby has 10 fingers and 10 toes and looks normal. But the birth of a defective infant or a stillbirth creates an entirely different emotional climate.

Unless we are a parent of a handicapped child, or have a vocational interest in the needs of handicapped persons, normality is something we are apt to take for granted, and we forget that "Those who are maimed or marred, visibly in form or face, lopped, lopsided or scarred, would consider it wonderful simply to be whole and straight."

There is a story about a small boy sitting at the breakfast table when his father was about to open his school report. Bracing himself up, he said, "Dad, before you read my school report I would like to ask you a question."

"Very good, my boy, what do you want to know?" was the reply.

" Well, Dad, I don't think it is going to be a good report, but what I want to know is this: if it isn't a good one, do you think it is largely because of my heredity or my environment?"

Many of the handicaps are caused by genetic factors, but the environment plays an important part as well in the development and the abilities.

Right from the start, the environment for the handicapped child may be adverse, particularly where the handicap is spotted early. For example, would your reaction to the child be the same if you feared or were informed that your young son or daughter was mentally or physically handicapped, compared to the healthy progression and confirmation of a normal offspring? I'm sure it wouldn't be.

When the handicap is recognised at birth or soon after, the doctor and nurse are faced with the prospect of informing the parents, if the mother has not already recognised the condition. There are no doubts that some doctors and nurses are ill-prepared to deal with this situation and may evade the issue for as long as they can. Even when the parents are informed, the information may be given in such a negative way that the shock and anxiety they experience is accentuated.

Parents at this crucial period need help to understand the problem and to help their child gain his full potential. Instead, they are often left in a vacuum until the child reaches school age, and by that time they, the parents, have adopted their own approach, which may be over-protective, or they may reject the child partially or completely. Relatives or friends might advise admission to an institution, or the mother may be cajoled into caring for a severely handicapped child at home when she is over-stressed and no help is forthcoming. And yet, as stated in the Encyclopaedia Britannica, "The handicapped are a normal part of today's society and do not exist as a group with separate lives. Theirs needs and rights are the same as those of any other person; their problems are the problems of all people and should be considered as part of the whole society."

Parents of severely handicapped children require considerable assistance and, as soon as possible, the child should be admitted to a day care unit. At this time, severely and profoundly handicapped children were not entitled to school education. In Edinburgh we had a combined day care and short stay residential unit. The combined unit had many advantages, as the child was familiar with the surroundings and staff, communication with the parents was on a daily basis and short stay residential arrangements could easily be accessed, whether for a vacation for the parents or as a babysitting service. It was also more economical to operate, and staff could share in training programmes and staffing substitutes.

The unit at Willowbrae House could take 29 children from 10 a.m. to 3:45 p.m., and we found that there was a tremendous advantage in having the children in the unit five days a week. The children received much more stimulation than they would at home, essentially because the nursing staff had more time to devote than the parents, and, in mixing with the other children at play with their toys, etc., much more opportunity was given to their development.

Prior to January 1963, we operated the unit on a part-time basis with restricted hours, and after changing to full-time the number of applications for attendance at the day care unit suddenly increased so that we finished with a waiting list of

30, and eventually had to expand the unit to take another 50 children. The demand for short stay residence dropped; obviously the parents found that with the extra relief during the day they were better able to manage at weekends and at night.

Willowbrae House was blessed with devoted and competent staff, and it was always a delight to visit. Moreover, they were another excellent source of information on parental needs and wishes. Even the children greeted me on my visits to show me their toys, etc., and it was encouraging to observe how quickly they responded to a stimulating programme, and the happy relationship they had with the staff.

Another facet in the care of these children is the effect on the other children of the family. If the mother can get relief during the day, she can devote more time to the others and to some extent reduce any jealousy or friction that might arise.

On reaching adult life, the mentally handicapped person needs an occupation that should help him or her feel independent and useful. We modified two schools which had been replaced by the Education Department, and established one as an occupation centre for the more severely handicapped, and the other at Longstone as a sheltered workshop operating on outside contracts.

Soccer was a popular interest of the trainees at the Longstone workshop, some of whom were remarkably skilled at the game. Matches were arranged from time to time against similarly interested groups and organisations. On one occasion the staff of the City Public Health Department was challenged to a match, and thus in September 1966 I foolishly agreed to act as referee. Amongst the spectators was one of the Down's syndrome boys from the workshop. On disagreeing with one of my decisions, he called out excitedly for all to hear, " Kill the referee, the man's an idiot!"

For the physically handicapped, a very progressive and active workshop was in operation at Simon Square, organized by the Edinburgh Cripple Aid Society. Miss Jean Waterston,

CITY OF EDINBURGH PUBLIC HEALTH SOCCER TEAM

the chief motivator and organiser of industrial type of work for the centre, led a team of energetic occupational therapists.

However, when we viewed the need to work more closely with other voluntary organisations, the multiplicity of organisations provided a major stumbling block. In Edinburgh we had 33 voluntary and professional associations concerned with the welfare of the disabled. In addition, there were 23 statutory bodies with similar or related interests and responsibilities. To add to the difficulties, it was found that many associations were aspiring to the same ends, and if these aspirations were to be achieved on an individual basis, there was a danger of conflict and unnecessary competition. One of the best examples of this was in the question of sheltered workshop provision which was planned separately for spastics, epileptics, mentally ill and mentally handicapped, to name only a few.

An effort was made in 1962 to get the voluntary committees together, but without success. It was only after the inception of the National Help the Disabled Week in 1963 that we made progress.

The voluntary and statutory bodies had to combine to plan the arrangements for this week and subsequently it was agreed to continue as a Committee for the Co-ordination of Services for the Disabled.

It was also clear from the start that such a large representative organisation would soon flounder unless mutually helpful activities were established, and it was also necessary to avoid friction between the various organisations by appointing a tactful chairman and neutral secretary. A constitution was drawn up and four sub-committees were appointed to carry out the real work of the committee. These sub-committees were made responsible for Sheltered Work, Welfare, Public Relations, and Sports and Recreation. The chairmanship of the main committee was in the able and tactful control of Dr. W.V. Anderson, an orthopaedic surgeon.

Was the effort worth while? There was no doubt that from its inauguration, more was achieved collectively through the Co-ordinating Committee than could have been contemplated by individual associations. The Welfare Sub-Committee, made up of social workers from most of the organisations, met each month. It served not only as a valuable forum for the interchange of information, and for discussion of individual problems, but was able to give increasing attention to many of the matters of importance to the welfare of disabled persons of all categories. For example, housing for the disabled was a recurring problem, and a close and friendly relationship was established with the Housing Department of Edinburgh Corporation, making that department much more aware of the problems.

Another part of the work was the publication of a Guide Book for Disabled Residents and Visitors to the City. The Girl Guide Association and Student Occupational Therapists helped to collate the information, and it was edited and published by the Scottish Tourist Board. Various sports activities were organised, and an important feature was the training sessions of coaches to make them aware of the needs of the disabled.

The handbook for general practitioners and other professional workers published by the Medical Advisory Co-ordinating Committee was updated and new material added to the fourth edition. The title was changed to "Index of Facilities for Mental Health Problems, and the Care of the Young and Old Chronic Sick and Handicapped".

The chairmanship of the Sheltered Work Sub-Committee was put on my shoulders. This was a big committee with over thirty members and with representation from the Health and Social Work professions, the Chamber of Commerce, the Unions, the Ministry of Labour, the Voluntary Associations, and from the Welfare Committee of Edinburgh Corporation. The first requisite was to ascertain the scope of the problem, and to establish the number of disabled persons who were capable of sheltered work.

The Ministry of Labour provided an analysis of the unemployed registered severely disabled persons in the city, but it was agreed that this was not enough because of the complexity of the problem. It was agreed to approach the Department of Social Medicine, University of Edinburgh, with a view to compiling a register. This resulted in a pilot study of the records of the disabled in Edinburgh.

Among the conclusions and recommendations of the pilot study was that the record system of the various organisations had evolved with different ends in view, and contained a variable amount of disparate information. Nevertheless, it was possible to obtain basic identifying data and, in addition, a diagnosis of the type of disability. It was recommended that a central register should be established.

By July 1964 the main committee agreed that the voluntary agencies should start planning a register, and advice on a permanent record card was sought from the University Department.

The full report of the Sheltered Work Sub-Committee was

submitted in November 1965.

In addition to the central register, the sub-committee recommended the building of a workshop which would initially employ 50 disabled persons, with provision for future extension, and it was suggested that several industrial members of the Rotary Club be co-opted. Home-bound occupation and vocational training were also recommended. It was concluded that the sub-committee should continue to ensure that recommendations were met.

Finally, about 1500 pounds was raised to produce a film and exhibition stand to illustrate the value and importance of co-ordination. These projects were later presented at the Congress of the International Society for the Rehabilitation of the Disabled, which was held in Wiesbaden, Germany in 1966.

While some form of occupation is necessary for the handicapped, whether in sheltered work or in regular industry, the need for special housing is also important.

Many handicapped adults manage to work in occupation centres or sheltered work, only because they have the shelter, support and understanding they require from their parents or relatives. Take away their home, and their world collapses about them. Even where home conditions are not entirely satisfactory, the handicapped person should not be removed from the environment in which they are happy, or relatively happy, to the expensive hospital or institutional provision which they do not require.

For those already in hospital or institution, many could be living in the community if adequate services were provided. Nevertheless we do a great disservice to handicapped persons in institutions if we discharge them into a community which lacks the support services.

Clearly, these problems must be looked at within the general context of the services provided and, at the same time, the order of priorities must be recognised. In consequence, we were under considerable pressure to provide a half-way type of hostel to help integrate mentally handicapped persons, from the hospital to the community. Successful rehabilitation would result in that person becoming a national asset instead of a liability.

In November 1963 we opened a hostel for employable mentally handicapped males. Eversley House was in its own grounds in a good residential area, and had accommodation for 17 residents and residential staff. Each potential resident was initially screened by the hospital doctor, or family doctor, and then interviewed by the disablement resettlement officer from the Ministry of Labour Industrial Rehabilitation Unit (I.R.U.), following which the medical officer from my department and the hostel warden assessed the resident.

The handicapped person was usually admitted to the hostel a week or two before starting an intensive training programme at the I.R.U. to help him acclimatise himself. Thereafter, on completion of the course the resident was started in employment.

At the hostel, training was given on handling money and budgeting, and on all other requirements necessary for life in lodgings. For the illiterate, voluntary classes were held on a regular basis. Few restrictions were applied, other than the general disciplines required by society. About 9 to 10 months after starting work, the resident left the hostel to return to his own home or to suitable lodgings. He was, however, encouraged to visit the hostel regularly, particularly in the evenings or weekends. Many of the discharged residents did this to watch TV, to seek advice, or just to meet and talk to new residents.

In five years we had 79 admissions plus three re-admissions. The shortest stay was for one week and the longest for 2 1/2 years. Forty-seven of the 79 admissions were from our hospital for the mentally handicapped (Gogarburn); 13 were admitted from their own homes and the remainder came from other authorities or hospitals. Only 13 residents were regarded as failures. Over 40 residents were able to live independent lives, all of them in full-time employment.

When one is immersed in all these developments it is easy to become complacent or preoccupied with local concerns, and to ignore advances or experiences elsewhere. Fortunately there was ample opportunity to keep abreast of national and international services. Firstly, my colleagues in the university helped to keep me informed, or to refer me to the current publications, and we had many fruitful conversations over a meal in the staff dining-room. Contacts were also developed with other professionals working in the same field, and in other parts of Britain.

At a national level, I was appointed to a committee "to consider and report on the existing practices in relation to the residential care of children in the care of local authorities and voluntary organisations, who suffer from physical, mental or emotional handicap or disability". In this capacity I was able to visit facilities in a number of authorities.

Another very interesting meeting was a study group on paediatric aspects of severe mental handicap, held at Willoughby Hall, Nottingham, in 1969. The study group was organised by the Spastic Society, who invited a wide range of disciplines and interests all properly concerned with the problems of subnormality. Papers had to be pre-circulated so that when presenting the paper, the speaker could quickly go over the main points and direct attention to those which specially merited review. We met for five days and at the end we were admitted to the prestigious Carnation Club. I can't remember the significance of the carnation, but the ladies received blue silk scarves with a scattering of small carnations printed on them; the men received ties of the same colour with the carnations.

Another of the highlights of my career was the award I received from the Council of Europe. The fellowship was to study the Community Services for Mentally Disordered and Physically Handicapped and, in particular, to ascertain the methods and problems of rehabilitation and sheltered employment as they were experienced in Denmark and Holland. I had two weeks in each country as their guest, with a pre-arranged itinerary. At the end I had to submit a report to the Secretariat of the Council of Europe, with a copy to St. Andrew's House, Edinburgh (the Scottish department of the National Government), and to the Edinburgh Corporation.

Clearly, I was anxious to compare the services in Edinburgh with the services in these countries, and I was also certain that there would be considerable benefit in meeting and discussing mutual problems with colleagues in these countries, who were generally regarded as leaders in the services for handicapped persons. Of even more personal import was the need to get more information on the question of employing persons with a variety of handicaps in sheltered conditions, as plans were well advanced for the establishment of a large workshop in Edinburgh. It is true that international comparisons can be invidious and misleading, primarily because of different social histories and cultural approaches. Nonetheless, it was also clear that we had much in common.

Hence, on the 21st September 1967, I set sail from Harwich to Esbjerg in Denmark. Immediately there was an introduction to a different cultural approach. In the area of food, I found that Danes live to eat, while Britishers eat to live. On board ship I confused the appetiser with the main course, and when the main dish arrived I was sure it had to be shared with the Danish gentleman who shared my table. However, he assured me that the entire dishfull was for my consumption. Thereafter, I was prepared for self-indulgence.

At the seaport, two Danish senior government officials met me and they became my guides and friendly companions for the duration of my stay. We had an extensive schedule and very frank and open discussion with staff. Similar arrangements were made for me in Holland.

Everywhere I was received with utmost kindness and at

times with overwhelming hospitality. Everyone, regardless of his or her status within the service, was most willing to give time and thought to my questions and to show me the disadvantages as well as the advantages of the department or establishment or programme.

The most outstanding impression gained from this tour was the success of services where they were planned on a regional basis with no division between hospital and community services, or between medical and social services. The services for the physically and mentally handicapped in Denmark were comprehensive and alive to the needs of handicapped persons and their families; while the purposeful approach to the occupational needs of the handicapped in Holland could not be surpassed.

My tour in the Netherlands covered a variety of workshops, each with different problems, but with the same emphasis on making full use of the capacities of handicapped persons. The workshops, or social workshop in Holland, not only made complete use of available manpower, but also gave the disabled self-respect and encouraged independence. It was also possible to confirm that persons with a variety of handicaps can work amicably and effectively within this setting, provided sensible arrangements are made in the workshop. An example of these integrated workshops can best be illustrated by my visit to Dordrecht. At that time this was the biggest workship in the Netherlands, employing approximately 850 handicapped persons and about 100 staff. It served a population of about 300,000, twenty-six percent of the workers were mentally handicapped, ten percent mentally ill, and the rest physically handicapped. There was some degree of segregation of the handicapped, but it should be realised that the level of handicap in some areas was quite severe.

One area was occupied by a number of workers who were suffering from Down's syndrome, working on a production line producing TV sets. The general administrative and clerical departments had a good proportion of former mental hospital patients.

The workshop had a special training centre where the intelligence, co-ordination, concentration and aptitude of the individual could be assessed before he or she entered a department.

A paramount factor for success in any workshop for the handicapped is the calibre and experience of the Director and his staff. Obviously, large units can attract good salaries, can command better staff for the posts, and are economically more viable. Apart from their technical abilities, the staff in these units require psychological insight as well as the ability to relate production needs to the capabilities and temperaments of the disabled. Staff/employee ratios varied between 1:10 and 1:14. While I was in Holland I was fortunate to be given plans of the workshop at Alkmaar, which I thought would be helpful to our own architect; it was designed for a similar population to our proposed workshop.

This travelling fellowship would have been futile and wasteful of time and energy if no action were taken to gain from the experience.

Therefore, six specific recommendations were included in the report; these incorporated a regional planning committee with representation from the local authorities from Edinburgh and its environs, the Regional Hospital Board, and voluntary organisations. It is perhaps a worthy ending to this chapter to include one of the verses taken from the Canadian Official Song for the International Year of the Disabled Persons 1981, entitled "Look Beyond" and written by a disabled person:

"I need so much more than sheltered employment,
I need less than pity or tears;
I need your respect and I need your compassion,
Oh lend me your eyes and your ears.

Then see me and touch me, and feel as I feel,
Hear what I say, can't you see I am real,
Look beyond what I am not
And you will see just what I am;
I'm a woman, I'm a child, I'm a man."

CHAPTER 10

HOPES THAT VANISH

Early in July 1965 I attended a seminar at the Tavistock Institution of Human Relations, London, organised by Professor Gerald Caplin of Boston, U.S.A. I had read a number of his publications and was extremely interested in his views. The subject on this occasion was "Public Health Psychiatry and Preventive Intervention".

Following this seminar I submitted a report to Edinburgh Corporation, suggesting the establishment of an experimental unit which would be responsible for providing a multi-disciplinary service, particularly during crises periods. Permission was granted to prepare a detailed scheme, and this was presented to the Corporation in the autumn of 1965.

The plan was drawn up with the help of Wallace McCulloch, a psychiatric social worker from Bradford University, previously at Edinburgh University, and a number of other colleagues. The key elements were in the writings of Professor Gerald Caplin: the need for the integration of services on a multi-disciplinary basis, the inter-relationship of medical and social factors, and on the theory that within a given urban area there is a close correlation between certain indices of medical, psychological and social disorder.

It is widely known that there are groups of people within most communities who present more medical and social problems than others, and we know that many of these problems emanate from disturbed family relationships, child neglect, poor housing conditions, unemployment and other forms of financial distress, below-average intelligence, and isolation. It is also known that many people who are emotionally distressed may present this in the form of physical illness or, conversely, in symptoms of social malaise. It had also been demonstrated that communities with a low degree of social organisation also appear to have high rates of mental and social problems.

One of the greatest barriers to progress in social work and social medicine practice has been the fragmentary attack on social and medico-psychological problems, dictated by the particular and sometimes limited interests of the various social and medical agencies. The result of this piecemeal approach was, and still is, a limited impact on the variety of involved factors, and a complexity of services so bewildering that the person needing support, and who needs it quickly, does not know where to go to get the most effective help.

Intervention and early support during a period of crisis is important, especially since persons whose whole life situation is punctuated by periods of stress which are onerous, are more willing to accept advice and help during an acute phase.

Following discussions with the Edinburgh Medical Research Council, we divided the city of Edinburgh into 23 voting districts and looked at the social indices per 1000 persons at risk in each area. We found that St. Giles and Craigmillar Districts competed with one another for top place with the highest rates of juvenile delinquency, attempted suicide, children in care, evictions, overcrowding, infant mortality, gynaecological conditions, venereal disease, and geriatric hospital admissions.

St. Giles District was in an old established central area of the city, containing the majority of lodging houses and vagrant population, and consequently we felt it would not be a good area for an experiment of this nature. On the other hand, Craigmillar was a district developed before 1939, but with poor housing and low socio-economic conditions, and was a community with a low degree of social organisation.

During our discussions it became apparent that we could perhaps use these districts as a means of measuring the success or failure of the centre, by the possible change in rank compared with the other precincts. It was also clear that measurement of the success or failure should be assessed, not by the participants but by an outside body, and approaches were made to the university.

The name given to the Centre was similarly considered carefully as it was deemed to be rash to call it a "Mental Health Centre" in view of the stigma still attached to the word "Mental". Likewise, the titles "Health Centre" and "Social Work Centre" did not, in our opinion, meet the desired requirements. These latter titles implied that the client or patient was able to decide between health and social needs. In some cases, similar centres have been called "Family Welfare Centres", but this title could discourage the single person or someone who decided that his or her personal problem had no connection with the family. We concluded that most people would divide their problems into three categories, namely Health, Welfare and Advice. Consequently it was decided to use this triad to name the centre, not only because the interpretation should cover the majority of personal problems, but it was also sufficiently anonymous to prevent attachment of any form of stigma.

While the problems of dealing with client or patient issues when they arise are of undoubted importance, the prevention of breakdown must be the *sine qua non* of any such establishment or service, and the operational arrangements must be studied as well. There is a need, therefore, to make use of people who can spot early signs of trouble, i.e., health visitors, district nurses, school teachers, religious leaders, club leaders, bar attendants, voluntary workers, etc. In a study carried out about this time in Edinburgh, the use of health visitors in preventive geriatrics had shown that they could spot at an early stage elderly patients requiring therapeutic action.

Reference has also been made to the fact that poor social organisation in a community leads to social problems. For this reason, and just before the centre was ready for opening, we called a public meeting. The panel comprised heads of city departments, a police superintendent and representatives from the city's Health and Welfare Committees; I chaired the meeting. The meeting was widely advertised, but in spite of this a poor public attendance was anticipated. To our complete surprise we had an overflow meeting.

The audience was given details of the proposed centre as well as the reasons and aims of the centre. Caplin has always recommended that to provide change in a community, one must seek out the leaders, whether law-abiding or not, and help them to establish the necessary changes. The audience was challenged to set up a community organisation, and during question time two hot issues were raised. Why was there a lack of public telephones, and why had Edinburgh Corporation failed to provide adequate day care facilities?

In answer to the first issue, the assembly was asked if they had taken any steps to bring the problem to the attention of the telephone company. The answer was no. Then it was suggested that this kind of problem could be channelled through the type of community organisation we were suggesting.

We were taken aback by the second question. The Corporation had recently built a new children's day care unit, only to have it destroyed by vandals. Why should we build another one, and what guarantees would there be that a new facility would be protected against destruction? The answer: "We, the community, did not ask for the original one nor was it located in the right area. If they were consulted, the locals would ensure its continued existence."

A Community Council was subsequently formed comprising local leading citizens, including a known criminal leader.

Apart from finding suitable accommodation, the setting up of an inter-disciplinary centre, which represented several departments and voluntary agencies, required a considerable amount of groundwork. The proposal for the centre was made towards the end of 1965, but the facility wasn't opened until March 1968.

The Co-ordinator was appointed in November 1967, and immediately had to consult with the Medical Research Council regarding the organisation of a systematic recording of data which would be useful not only to the centre, but also to the research teams.

The next step was to assemble staff to discuss the aims and objectives of the centre as well as the proposed operation. The local general practitioners, the headmasters of the local schools, and the local religious leaders were all invited to the centre before it opened, and very useful discussions ensued.

The aims of the new Health, Welfare and Advice Centre were summarised as follows:

1. To provide a simple integrated service to meet
    the social and medico-psychological needs of
    the district with a particular bias towards early
    intervention during crisis periods;
2. To encourage positive community action which
    may lead to better social integration and
    healthier attitudes;
3. To conduct operational research.

The centre was situated in a Council building owned by the city and within easy reach of most parts of the district. When the centre opened, the staff consisted of the following:

*   The Centre Co-ordinator – who was a Senior
    Social Worker
*   Four Child Care Officers
*   Psychiatrist (part-time)

- Mental Health Officers (one full-time, one part-time)
- Three Health Visitors
- A Medical Social Worker
- Probation Officers (part-time)
- A Marriage Guidance Counsellor (part-time)
- Prevention of Cruelty to Children Inspector (part-time)
- Citizen's Advice Bureau Volunteers
- Clerk/Receptionist

To avoid relative isolation and potential rivalry in the centre among the various professions, we made sure that all the offices had a mixture of staff.

Within a very short time we had to provide a substantial increase in staff, as well as two Little Sisters of the Assumption, a community worker, and a rent collector who dealt only with families referred to him by the social worker. The psychiatrist, although part-time, had to take cases and support and advise staff. Caplin had stressed repeatedly that the psychiatrist's role is more effective indirectly by consultation than by direct therapeutic action, but this would take time to prove and at least initially, he was involved directly in some therapy.

It was originally anticipated that the reception area would be served by a receptionist who would be responsible for receiving enquiries, for making appointments and possibly for some clerical work. She would also be able to give general information to enquirers. It was also hoped that each person would be initially interviewed by a trained social worker. Experience proved that these ideals were impractical, and we had to call on the volunteers from the Citizens' Advice Bureau for help in dealing with the pressure at reception.

One important factor overlooked initially was the need to give more consideration at the top for the official Corporation policy, which may not always be seen by those who serve it to be in accord with a community's needs. Where this occurred there was a need for discussions with the principal officers so that we could learn from the experience of such an experimental unit, and advise the administration.

Obviously, when several local authority departments are involved there is suspicion and rivalry over the final administrative responsibility. My Chief, Dr. H. Seiler, who supported and advised me throughout, was given the authority, as the Health Department had borne the major part of the cost and the planning. Nevertheless, responsibility for the general supervision of the scheme was governed by a joint Health, Welfare and Children's Sub-Committee of the Corporation.

In the first year of operation there was an increase from 40 clients per week when the centre started to 200 clients per week at the end of the year. The rate for children coming into care of the local authority fell from 22.2 to 16.9 per thousand persons at risk. However, it was felt that this required examination over an extended period, as a few of the other districts had a small reduction. The police reported a drop in crime in the area.

Within a few months of our opening, a group of mothers, with the help of the Co-ordinator and the health visitors, had set about organising a play centre with a donation of toys from the Scottish prisons. The premises in which they held their evening meetings were also soon in demand by local groups to organise an arts festival and other community activities. In fact, so great were the efforts to organise activities, in spite of the total lack of facilities, that a grant was awarded by the Gulbenkian Foundation for the employment of a community worker. Plans were also made for a new day care centre.

Just as we were getting excited at the potential for the community as well as the research benefits, the National Government dropped a major bombshell. Having transferred responsibility for Community Mental Health Services from the Welfare Department to the Health Departments in 1960, it was decided to give it back to Welfare in 1969. Why?

The "Younghusband Report on Social Work and the Community", which was the basis for the government's action, stated in paragraph 9 of the report that local authority attempts at co-ordination were not entirely satisfactory, and even where they worked well were costly in working time. It also stated in the next paragraph, "In order to provide better services and to develop them economically, it seems necessary that local authority services designed to provide community care and support whether for children, the handicapped, the mentally and physically ill, or the aged, should be brought within a single organisation." This paragraph went on to state the responsibilities of this organisation would be wide but it should only be based "on the insights and skills of the profession of Social Work."

This was completely contrary to the current views. The British Working Party Report on The Handicapped School Leaver emphasized that "disability" had medical, psychological and social components, but it was wrong if medical care alone were lavished on the physical defects without due weight being given to the social impact of the handicapped.

In another government paper, "Better Services for the Mentally Handicapped", it stated that "the resources of the Health Services, Personal Social Services and Education Services should be deployed in close and effective collaboration. Only if this is done can the relevant professional skills be most effectively used to provide complete and co-ordinated services."

Just prior to the enactment of the government bill, a convention was held in Peebles Hydro Hotel to consider the pros and cons for such action. I was privileged to present a paper entitled "Logical or Illogical?"

After highlighting some of the practical problems which would emerge if we separated medical and social services of the local authority, and contending that any move to separate the agencies would be a retrograde step, I looked closely at the arguments from both sides. Both agreed about the need for more integration. Wherein, therefore, lay the controversy? In a nutshell, the medical officers of health considered that a doctor should be the director of a combined service; the social workers, on the other hand, considered this would be a threat to their professional status and career structure, and were demanding their own department.

Both professions had a lot to contribute; both had a lot to gain by combining their services and energies in a multi-disciplinary team. I argued that the position of the Director of a combined department should be open to any professional worker, regardless of his or her particular discipline. The fact that one is a doctor, a social worker or a psychologist doesn't assume the competencies of an administrator.

Following the convention, I met with the Minister of Social Services, but it was too late to change government direction.

It is interesting to note that over the years we keep repeating the same mistakes. As far back as the first century A.D., the Roman author Gaius Petronius wrote:

> "We trained hard, – but it seemed that every time we were beginning to form into teams, we would be reorganised. I was to learn later in life that we tend to meet any new situation by re-organising – and a wonderful method it can be for creating the illusion of progress while producing confusion, inefficiency and demoralisation."

With the change in the administrative responsibility, the centre was replaced by a Social Work Area Office, and the other professionals and volunteers moved out, including the community worker funded by the Gulbenkian Foundation. Thus an experiment with open accessibility, professional and volunteer co-operation, and research potential was sacrificed for limited professional gain and by inept politicians.

The resultant setback to our plans and aspirations naturally made me look around for new opportunities and to consider my future role in the department, although there was now some talk about the reorganization of the Health Services.

While I was in this mood and cogitating the problem, a good friend, Dr. Peter Sykes, a psychiatrist, walked into my office with an offer to move to New Brunswick, Canada and take up the appointment of Director of Services for the Mentally Retarded for the province. He was in Britain to recruit psychiatrists. At the time Canada was far from my thoughts. The offer was a three-year contract, and following a period of serious contemplation and discussion with my wife and family, we decided to take the plunge.

Perhaps the most pleasant memory I have of this time is the banquet held for me in the Grand Hall at Craighouse Hospital, and arranged by Edinburgh Corporation and the Royal Edinburgh Hospital Board. In addition to representatives from these august bodies there were friends and colleagues from the university, the voluntary agencies, and members of my own department.

I had no way of knowing much about the weather or life in Canada, nor did I realise how truly the poem, prepared by Dr. Jim Affleck for the occasion, depicted the environment. It was entitled "The Emigrant":

"*When New Brunswick snow surrounds your wooden hoose,*
And bear and elk and mink and moose,
All bark and call – like hell let loose,
Remember (in spite o' calliper and chair),
The welcome's always warm at Simon Square

When western sun has browned New Brunswick grass,
And lakes and fields are hard and parched,
And heat's oppressive – and each task a menace,
Remember – the breeze is always cool on Johnston Terrace

When Yankee tongues grate in your ear,
And palate's tired o' wersh Canadian beer,
Remember, – though some folk are sick and queer
And paranoid, – and cast discretion to the wide,
The coffee's always hot in Morningside"

Footnote: Simon Square was the centre for physically handicapped; Johnston Terrace refers to the health department; Morningside is The Royal Edinburgh Hospital.

CHAPTER II

OVER THE SEA - TO WHAT!

It was late March 1970, Prestwick Airport was bathed in bright sunshine, the daffodils were blooming, and the surrounding countryside looked fresh, verdant and vibrant as we boarded an Air Canada Boeing 707 for Montreal.

Our son, who had never flown before, felt sick, but this was soon overcome when he was invited into the cockpit to meet the pilot and receive some souvenirs of his flight. Our daughter was at the start of her Easter vacation, so she accompanied us with a view to enrolling at New Brunswick University.

In contrast to Prestwick, Montreal looked grim; a blizzard was blowing and everything was covered in a thick white blanket of snow. Because of the weather, our connecting flight to Fredricton had been cancelled and we had to stay the night in the Hilton Hotel.

To us, the warmth of the hotel was oppressive, and we had to share a bedroom with the children. We decided to have a light meal before retiring and ordered chicken sandwiches. The waitress asked, "Hot or cold?" We pointed out to her that we weren't very hungry as we had eaten a lot on the plane. Still, a hot sandwich sounded appetizing, so we ordered it. Next we were presented with a salad, which we assumed would be eaten with the sandwich. The sandwiches didn't appear and while we waited, we proceeded to munch on the salad. When finished, the plates were removed and we looked with alarm at the hot chicken sandwich.The large plate was covered in bread and chicken, and to add to our perplexity, the plate was accompanied by a large bowl of french fries. Do all Canadians eat such big meals?

We had to be at the airport early next morning and, at that time of the morning, the continental breakfast was coffee and doughnuts. While we waited for our transport we decided to walk outside. Dressed only in our British overcoats, we weren't prepared for the severe cold and chilling wind. The security guard thought we were crazy and ordered us back inside. Our little black poodle dog accompanied us, but we didn't see him until we boarded our flight to Fredericton. The plane was much smaller than our Boeing 707, and the dog was in a compartment at the back of the passenger section. He kept howling and barking until, in exasperation, our son was allowed by the attendant to join him.

On arrival at Fredericton airport we were met by Peter, and as we drove into town we were transfixed by the view around us. The St. John River ice was breaking up, and huge thick lumps of ice with white tops and bright aquamarine-coloured bases were scattered on the banks of the river, while many more of the ice floes moved down the fast-flowing water. The houses looked different, either in wood or with siding – no slate roofs – and the grass was brown, not with the "Western Sun" but with the severe frost and chill. The deciduous trees were like skeletons against the brilliant blue sky which appeared to be at a greater height than what we had been used to, and the green spruce trees provided the only other colour, although even the green looked lifeless.

We stayed with Peter and Jean Sykes for a few weeks until we could purchase a home. It was quite exciting to be taken around the Canadian houses by the real estate people, although

I had trouble removing my shoes every time we entered a home, then to put them on again to face the slush and dirt. Finally, we settled on a new home on the side of a hill overlooking the St. John River valley.

The St. John River runs to the town of St. John and ends in the Reversing Falls. The river runs into a gorge formed by limestone cliffs, and when the tide is going out it drops eleven feet to sea-level. At high tide the flow is in the opposite direction and there is increased turbulence during these changes.

When we first went out for supper with Jean and Peter we found that the liquor laws in the province were an anomaly. We had wine with our meal and continued chatting over coffee. The restaurant wasn't busy so we decided to continue our chit-chat over some drinks, called the waiter over to be informed that we could not have drinks because we were not consuming food. We also found that one could not order a drink at the bar then carry it to the table – it had to be carried by the waiter.

Another aberration was registration with the College of Physicians and Surgeons. Each province had different conditions: in this case I was allowed to practise my profession as long as I was employed by the provincial government.

Then my first Canadian car was purchased, a Ford Fairlane with a powerful V-8 engine; after a few weeks my daughter and I had to sit our provincial driving test. It was thrilling to drive a new car with a vigorous engine on wide uncongested roads, but at times disconcerting to discover that the beautifully paved road could suddenly change to gravel road and, after a few miles, unexpectedly return to a smooth highway. It was one way of reminding voters they were in the riding of the opposition member of the legislature.

Our container with all our furniture and worldly possessions arrived safely soon after, and we had to get the customs officer to come to the house to break the customs seal before unloading the contents into our house. He appeared to be interested only in our garden equipment; we were relieved as we were shocked to find that all the leftover booze from our farewell party had been packed.

Once settled in our new home, our daughter approached the university about starting her teaching course in the fall session. However, in the end she decided to complete her teacher's course at Murray House, Edinburgh. Thereafter, she had a wonderful time flying back and forth between Edinburgh and New Brunswick on her vacations, and being fitted out each time with the latest Canadian fashion clothes.

When she returned for her Christmas break, she left Britain during a strike by electrical union workers, with almost black-out qualities, and flew over Fredericton illumined by masses of coloured lights which decorated the exterior of the homes as well as the spruce trees. It was like arriving in Fairyland.

Her summer vacation which followed was equally exciting when she again saw the landscape from the air - this time from a parachute. With a group of students she received some train-ing from the army at Gagetown, and for her first jump we went to the airport at Houlton, in Maine, U.S.A. With a great deal of apprehension we watched from the airstrip when she dropped from the plane, she was first out; great relief when we saw the parachute open, but then concern and anxiety when at about 500 feet she was blown off course, and landed in the forest several miles from the expected landing strip. Fortu-nately, army helicopters were standing by, and she was soon restored to us. Her next jump was perfect.

Meanwhile our son attended the local school. His first day was a bit of an embarrassment as he attended in his Edinburgh school uniform, which looked foreign to the local pupils. A few weeks later we were very surprised when he returned home and announced that he had been picked to play on the school ice hockey team. "But you can't skate," was our imme-diate response. However, he assured us that he would be given lessons.

Having rigged him out in all his hockey kit, we went to the local ice hockey arena to watch him play. The school team emerged to the cheers of parents and pupils. Somehow Iain remained upright, he even managed to skate across the arena. However, when faced with the goalkeeper and the puck at his stick, the effort to propel the little black disc was too much – his legs moved in different directions and he collapsed on the ice. This had been his first time on skates. His teacher had wrongly assumed he was experienced just like all his schoolmates, and the promised lessons had not materialised.

Still, in the summer he was expert in swimming at Mactaquac Lake, just north of Fredericton, and proved to be very proficient as a sailor on our neighbour's yacht. Indeed, it didn't take him long to be competent in all of the Canadian sporting events.

My introduction to the Department of Social Services and Community Health was reassuring, as my boss was the Deputy Minister, Dr. Graham Clarkson, a Glasgow graduate, and the department's Financial Officer, Dugal Richford, was also from Glasgow. Dr. Peter Sykes was in the department as well.

Soon after my initiation I was to make my first mistake. I was asked to represent the department at a meeting at Dalhousie University, and was given the appropriate papers. On returning home I studied the map in order to locate Dalhousie, New Brunswick. Very early next morning I set off and arrived around lunchtime to find a small town with stinking odours from the pulp mill, and no evidence of a university.

While having lunch I asked the waitress about the university.

"What university?" was her reply.

I said, "Dalhousie University, of course, where is it?"

"We don't have a... there is a Dalhousie University in Halifax, Nova Scotia, but not here."

Having driven over 200 miles, almost to the Gaspe Peninsula, I had to make the return journey with a feeling of embarrassment and confusion. Meanwhile, Dr. Clarkson had telephoned my wife to ask if I caught my flight, to which my wife assured him I had set off in plenty of time to drive there. Recognising my mistake, Dr. Clarkson was at my home to greet me on my return with a broad grin, and with a request to phone the university next day with an apology. Thereafter I attended several meetings at Dalhousie University and was frequently reminded of my mistake.

Another faux pas was at the annual meeting of the Mental Health Division at the University of Moncton. At this time I had assumed the additional duties of Director of Mental Health Services, as Peter had resigned about a year after my arrival in Canada. The meeting was attended by the Minister as well as a good representation from the provincial staff. It was a live-in for all of the participants, and the programme was arranged to encourage staff to work and play together. The programme lasted for three days and was a heavy one, beginning at 9:00 a.m. each morning and ending at 9:30 p.m. in the evening. However, the day did not end at that time, but continued often into the early hours of the morning. An excellent entertainment programme was organised by the staff, although one of the evening events almost ended in misadventure. A casino was set up with all the accoutrements of the trade, but bets were severely limited and in most cases fake money was used. To add to the excitement, two of the staff disguised as robbers appeared with toy guns. Unfortunately the university security guards also appeared on the scene and there was a tense moment when attempts were made to convince the guards that it was a prank.

Naturally, towards the end of the annual meeting all participants were feeling exhausted, and I was not an exception. I had chaired the meetings and presented my annual review of the Division. The final item on the agenda was a banquet with a guest speaker from the Department of National Health and

Welfare, Canada. In closing the meeting, and just prior to the banquet, I appealed to the members to take their rest, but not to be late for the banquet and our distinguished speaker. As a complementary piece of advice, I suggested that if they had concerns about oversleeping they should get someone to "knock them up". At this the whole audience was convulsed in laughter, much to my confusion until I learned that my last comment had a sexual connotation, unlike the British interpretation.

Yet another slip-up occurred, this time by my wife who is an excellent cook. We had been recipients of a very enjoyable social evening at Dr. Clarkson's home, and we responded by inviting the Clarkson family for supper. For dessert my wife made a " baked Alaska". She had read that it was possible to prepare the fruit and sponge base beforehand and freeze it. Later she added the ice-cream and meringue just before baking in the oven. While my wife was in the kitchen she was acutely aware of a sudden silence followed by some hilarity. Attempts to attack the frozen-solid base of the appetizing delicacy were proving to be almost futile and, when we found we were all in the same boat, we delighted in a variety of measures to resolve the problem. The event was enjoyed by all, and it helped to remove any reserves which might have existed.

Politics in New Brunswick were also practised differently from my experience in Britain. Soon after my arrival in Fredericton, Dr. Clarkson took me to a sitting of the Provincial Legislature. On several occasions I was very surprised by the unparliamentary language and name-calling which clouded the proceedings. Then early in 1971 at a government conference in the Beaverbrook Hotel, in fact the day after the Liberal Government was replaced by Conservatives, I was surprised by the glum and despondent demeanour of my colleagues. When questioned, they said that the change of government meant that all jobs were at risk. When I expressed surprise and disbelief, they queried my own situation. "I have a three-year contract," I replied with assurance. Was the contract based on a ministerial letter, was the next question. "Yes," I replied. Then it can be cancelled by the new minister, was the response. My composure was further undermined by newspaper reports of government layoffs.

However, my position was secure, but in April 1971 I learned with very deep regret that Dr. Clarkson was resigning as Deputy Minister to take up a new appointment at the University of Alberta. This was followed soon afterwards by the resignation of my good friend Dr. Peter Sykes, who returned to England.

Peter was appointed Director of Mental Health Services for the Province of New Brunswick in May 1969, and took up his duties in September of that year. He was instrumental in establishing the Mental Health Services on a regional basis and for the emphasis on community in mental health planning and practice. I was therefore very privileged to inherit a competent organisation.

The changes in the province resulted from a consultant's report. In 1969 Grunberg and M.D.T. Associates recommended a phased approach with the appointment of a Director of Mental Health, a Community Liaison Officer, a Director of Mental Retardation Programming responsible to the Director of the Division, and Director of Psycho-Social Research. A permanent Advisory Committee on Mental Health Services was also to be created.

At a regional level, five Regional Directors were appointed and regional Mental Health Centres developed. The terms of reference originally specified that the Regional Director must be a qualified psychiatrist if the region included a Provincial Mental Hospital among its facilities. In practice, it was found that administrative responsibilities consumed a considerable portion of the Director's time and conflicted with the psychiatrist's clinical interest. Consequently it was decided that the Regional Director should be a well-qualified administrator, preferably with some professional background. It was at the same time agreed that each region should have a senior psychiatrist appointed who could act as clinical and programme consultant to the Director.

In setting up the Division, two organisational patterns were compared. The first one was the central government agency in which the Provincial Department assumes responsibility for the delivery of all primary services, in addition to the establishment of legislation and development of the necessary fiscal and personnel resources. The primary advantage of this pattern was organisational efficiency. The disadvantage was less involvement in programme development by local professional workers and the community.

The second pattern was the looser pattern, with central government withdrawing from the provision of services in favour of a regional organisation. The advantage of this system was increased community interest and participation in the formulation of programmes; and the disadvantage was the vulnerability of the system to the nature of leadership provided.

We used a combination of both patterns, but weighted towards central government control. This pattern was adopted because of the initial need for provincial planning, co-ordination and utilisation of resources, as well as the need for reorientation of existing staff from the custodial approach to an emphasis on community care.

Associated with the regional organization was the need to review the role of the two provincial mental hospitals and the children's hospital at St. John.

The Provincial Mental hospital at St. John, which towered above the Reversing Falls of the St. John River, was old, outmoded and unsuitable for its purpose. It had 600 chronic patients as well as 116 beds assigned for the acute psychiatric unit. Preliminary plans were therefore drawn up for a gradual phasing out of this hospital; these included the provision of 40 acute beds in Fredericton and 60 new beds in Moncton, and the development of day hospitals and day care centres. Consequently in the fiscal year 1971-72 the following programme activities occurred:

- The Regional Centres gradually assumed responsibility for the screening of admissions to all provincial in-patient facilities.
- The hospitals were organized in sections: e.g., Acute Psychiatry, Geriatrics, Training and Rehabilitation, and Mental Retardation.
- Regional and Hospital Programme Advisory Committees were established.
- A Day Care Centre for adult patients and children with emotional problems opened in Fredericton in co-operation with the Canadian Mental Health Association.
- A new method of data collection was introduced.
- Patients in the Forensic Unit of St. John Hospital were transferred to a Maximum Security Unit in the Provincial Hospital, Campbellton.
- An Inter-departmental Committee for Mental Retardation was established.

The chronic population in the St. John Provincial Hospital had been divided into two groups – those in the Forensic Unit, i.e., those on Lieutenant Governor's Warrant, and a conglomeration of chronic psychotics, psycho-geriatric patients and mental retardation patients.

My first introduction to the Forensic Unit was spine-chilling; patients were continually confined in a ward with few recreational or other activities, and much of their time appeared to be spent walking round the ward. I sensed the need for urgent action.

Subsequently, we were able to find space at the Campbellton Provincial Hospital and plans were drawn up to provide maximum security for 50 patients. As part of the preparation I attended a conference for this type of patient, and also spent several days at a maximum security unit in Montreal. At this unit I was put in the care of a convicted murderer, and we became good friends as we viewed and discussed the various programmes offered by this facility. On our last day I posed the following question to him:

"If you were in my shoes and had to provide a foolproof method of security, what action would you take?"

He replied: "Before opening the facility I would divide your staff into two; one half would be patients, the other half staff. Operate the unit for a week, and I can assure you that at the end of that time someone will have found a weakness in your security."

I took his advice, and his recommendation proved to be correct. By the end of the week two major weaknesses were found, in spite of the earnest planning by staff and architects.

The date for the official opening of the Forensic Unit proved to be a disaster. It was March, and I had spent a few days with my family in Ottawa. On our way home we stopped for the night in Montreal. It was raining heavily when we retired, but in the morning when we drew back the drapes and looked out of the window we were faced by a high wall of snow. When we phoned the R.C.M.P. we were told that all the roads north and east of the city were blocked and it was impossible to get to Campbellton. The advice was to proceed as fast as possible through the States back to Fredericton. We took this advice.

Our drive along route 11 in Maine, U.S.A. was uneventful until we reached Knowles Corner when we approached an intersection. The main highway continued for several miles, then one had to backtrack along route 95 to Houlton. A secondary road, route 121, provided a faster approach, and as this road appeared to be in good condition we took it. For several miles we continued until we reached the top of a hill to find we were suddenly on a gravel road which was thick with slush and mud, high banks of snow lined our passage, and at times the road was limited to single lane.

We had a frightening and hazardous drive with the windscreen covered in mud, the car sliding and zigzagging, and the hilly and twisted road only adding to the difficulty of retaining control. Also, foremost on my mind was the danger of stalling the engine or stopping; with the mud and slush up to the running boards, it would have been impossible to get the car moving again.

Through this time the family sat tense and quiet except when they observed something requiring my attention, such as direction. When we got to the end of this "shortcut" we met a policeman who was very surprised to find that we had traversed that road. He said it was closed to traffic – we certainly had seen no cars, but then we hadn't seen any signs indicating the road was closed.

We reached the main highway to continue on to Houlton, which was free from snow; weather was mild and pleasant. We had supper then a short walk before resuming our journey, blissful in our thought that we had escaped the blizzard which we knew was moving in our direction.

But our optimism was short-lived. Scarcely out of the town when the blizzard struck, and we had to struggle on, sometimes following behind trucks or snow-ploughs in order to keep to the road. This in itself was sometimes dangerous, as it was dark and the snow frequently blotted out the rear or brake lights of the vehicles in front. With a great feeling of relief we arrived home, only to find our driveway covered in several feet of snow. I had to ram the car into the snow bank to get it off the road, and without unloading we wearily plodded through the snow and into the warm refuge of our home.

The Minister, who had arrived in Campbellton before the snow blizzard for the opening, was marooned there for a week, and the opening ceremony had to be cancelled.

Snow was a major problem in 1971. In March of that year it

was reported that we had the heaviest snowfall accumulation on record in the Fredericton area, with over 175 inches falling since the first flakes were recorded in October 1970. Even as the newspaper was reporting this record, a snowstorm was pelting some sections of the Maritimes with up to 14 inches of new snow.

Apart from the usual complication of heavy snowfalls, we were soon advised of the dangers of heavy deposits on the roof of our house, and more specifically, the problem of ice collecting under the snow when melting occurs as the temperature rises during the day. Consequently, we had to climb on to the roof armed with axes to break it up. This led to one alarming incident when we heard a yell and saw our son, Iain, disappear over the edge of the roof. Our distress turned to relief when we found him joyfully reposed on a soft bank of snow. It subsequently proved a popular site for regular roof-to-snowbank adventures. Another hazard was pockets of soft snow in the thick layers. It was not uncommon, especially for my wife, to suddenly sink up to her waist as we traversed what we thought was firmly packed snow. Because of this we bought snow-shoes, which required a particular skill to navigate.

Turning once more to the problems in the provincial mental hospitals, Grunberg and Associates reported the need to reduce overcrowding in St. John Provincial Hospital by developing a programme which would allow the placement of a large number of patients in the community. It was suggested that this could be achieved by developing a rehabilitation programme integrated with an extramural programme.

With the removal of the forensic unit there was some relief to the overcrowding, but we were still left with many chronic patients who had spent a long time in the institution. The new rehabilitation programmes in the hospital were helping, but we had a number of mentally handicapped residents who needed a programme to help them return to the community, to their own home, or to a hostel.

An associated problem was the number of mentally handicapped persons who had reached the age of 21 years or over, and were still living in the Hospital School for Children in Saint John. Apart from the fact that they were over the age when they logically should have left, it also meant that the efforts which had gone into their training had been wasted because of the lack of facilities to enable the adolescent or the adult to be trained for employment, either in sheltered work conditions or in open industry.

Fortunately a building at the St. Thomas University Complex, Chatham, became available which could provide residential accommodation for 120 to 150 residents. It was also possible to develop good workshop facilities, and assist the local community by providing extra places for those living at home, who were able to travel daily to the unit. In addition, arrangements were made with the local hospital for the provision of medical and/or nursing care, should this be required.

It is true that this approach could be regarded as a duplication of the institution, but it should be viewed within the existing problem. For example, we had a building which could readily be adapted and at the same time provide immediate relief to the hospitals. Moreover, the complex offered a constructive rehabilitation programme for the transition to planned community service.

A concomitant need was a new training programme for staff working in the field of the mentally handicapped. In March 1971 this programme was started, but soon after its inception the National Institute for Mental Retardation (N.I.M.R.) announced a new training programme and arrangements were made with the Department of Education to start a new course which was in line with the proposed Diploma Level I of the N.I.M.R. programme. Under this arrangement, staff were required to spend one year at the Technical College and successfully complete a Diploma I Level of training.

The Provincial Hospital in Saint John was described by Grunberg and Associates as "an eyesore even under very modest psychiatric standards, and should be abandoned as soon as is practicable." Consequently a meeting was held with the staff in January 1972 to develop a detailed plan outlining the problems relating to the phasing out of the building, and to provide recommendations for alternative facilities. In order not to adversely affect staff and patients, it was decided that deliberations should be kept confidential until definite plans had been made. The hospital population had declined from 1234 in 1967 to 716 in 1972, and the effect on staff morale, because of insecurity brought on by the new community developments and repeated public statements about the hospital's future or lack thereof, had a negative influence. Furthermore, with the phasing out of the acute unit, there was a danger of the hospital reverting to a custodial unit for chronically ill patients. This planning committee presented its report in April of that year, including twenty-five recommendations.

Another area which was of interest, but not the direct responsibility of the division, was the education and training of mentally handicapped children. Children who were described as educable mentally handicapped were educated within the school system, but those deemed to be trainable were dealt with under the Auxiliary Classes Act, with services provided by voluntary groups throughout the province. Our Children's Hospital in St. John was also involved in training.

In spring of 1971 the Minister of Education established a "Study Committee on Auxiliary Classes" to study operation of these classes and to make recommendations with respect to their future operation. I was the representative from the department, and it proved to be an interesting departure from problems and interests confined to the Mental Health Division. It also provided a wonderful opportunity to become conversant with the issues and people involved. The subsequent report was entitled "The Right to Choose" and "The Right to be Served", and was made public in the spring of 1973.

Sadly and reluctantly, I decided by the summer of 1972 that I could not continue to work under the political system which operated at that time. I also assumed that other provinces in Canada had similar problems, and consequently the decision was made to return to Britain. Had I known that the provincial political systems were different, or consulted with Dr. Clarkson or other colleagues in other provinces, I would most likely have stayed in Canada.

The thought of returning to Britain raised other considerations. In Britain the "Gray Paper on Management Arrangements for the Reorganized National Health Service" had been issued, and I realized it was necessary to be involved in the services before the new plans were implemented.

While contemplating my options, I saw an advertisement in one of the British medical journals for a post in the north-west of England which caught my attention. The appointment was for a consultant psychiatrist and medical administrator for Dovenby Hall Hospital, near Cockermouth. The hospital had 400 beds, and in addition to the hospital responsibilities, co-ordination of the service for the mentally handicapped in the Social Service Areas was also required. I submitted an application and was later scheduled, after an interview in England, to take up the appointment on November 1st, 1972.

Because of the need to get our son into the local school, my wife and son had to leave early and we had to arrange temporary accommodation. A complication was the family passport; they travelled with it, but on their arrival at Prestwick airport the passport officer refused admission to the country and threatened to send them back to Canada. We hadn't realized that both parents were required to accompany the child. Our son would have been quite happy to return to Canada, but fortunately, after some debate they were free to enter.

All our worldly goods were later packed into a container for shipment, but in the three months remaining to me I collected a number of keepsakes and memorabilia, surmising that we would not be returning to Canada. I had a relatively new Ford Galaxie, which was a full-size North American car. It was decided to take it back to Britain for touring, and I also anticipated using it to pull a trailer.

For this reason, and to allow me some time to spend on study and refreshing my mind on medications, etc., the journey home was made by sea. The ship was Polish, the *Stephan Batory*, which originated on the Clyde. It was an excellent means of relaxing and reviewing medical literature. It was also an experience to share thoughts and views with the Polish passengers on the ship. Anticipating a reluctance to discuss politics, I was surprised how free and open my shipmates were. For example, I had long discussions with the port manager for Gdynia, who was returning home after spending several months in the U.S.A. studying their management of seaports. I had to share a cabin with another Polish gentleman who engaged me in some serious conversations, even though he couldn't speak English and I had no knowledge of his language. I did, however, find that I could not share his love of vodka.

Travelling the Atlantic in late October, one could expect storms, but instead the weather was almost balmy with gentle sea swells, and it was often possible to sit on deck in a sheltered position. My experience in the St. Lawrence, on the other hand, was the reverse with cold winds and buffeting waves. Having a bath in these conditions meant restricting the amount of water – but that was only one of my concerns. The baths were located in the centre of the ship and one had to book a time. Entry was from the gents' washroom. While relaxing in my bath I noticed a second entrance, and being of an inquisitive nature, after I had dressed, proceeded through this other door only to find I was in the ladies' washroom.

Arriving in Southampton, I watched the unloading of my car, then walked into the customs shed. I was told to put all my goods on a table and had to empty my car, which was packed to capacity. The customs officer arrived and asked if I had anything to declare, whereupon, when I indicated the goods which were spread over two long tables, he exclaimed: "Are these all your goods?" and before I could reply, "How did you get them all here?" When I pointed out my car, he became more interested in it, and after a prolonged view of its attributes, decided that my possessions were of a personal nature and were within the tax limit and helped me repack the car – much to my relief as I had expected to pay a heavy duty on the goods.

And so I bade farewell to New Brunswick and to all our friends, never dreaming that I would be back there on a brief visit from Alberta in 1979 as a consultant, to give advice to the Provincial Planning Advisory Committee on Community Services for the Disabled.

CHAPTER 12

HOME AGAIN

The ancient town of Cockermouth is situated on the fringe of the Lake District National Park in North-West England. It lies at the mouth of the River Cocker where the River Derwent joins it. In contrast to the more wild and forested countryside of New Brunswick, the surrounding fields and hedges presented a more restful and pastoral setting.

The Poet Laureate William Wordsworth was born in Cockermouth and his home, a fine old Georgian house built in 1745, still stands in the main street. In the spring, thousands of daffodils line the roadside, and are a reminder of his well-known verse:

> *I wandered lonely as a cloud*
> *That floats on high o'er vales and hills,*
> *When all at once I saw a crowd,*
> *A host of golden daffodils.*

However, my approach to the town was not greeted by a colourful display but by grey overcast skies and drizzling rain, and driving my large American car proved quite a challenge in some of the narrow roads in the Lake District and elsewhere. On the other hand, it was exhilarating when on the motorway, especially when a smaller British car attempted to race me. Parking also presented a problem, and the car always attracted inquisitive viewers.

The hospital for the care of the mentally handicapped was situated in the village of Dovenby on the main road from Maryport to Cockermouth, and 26 miles distant from Carlisle. It had 400 beds to serve a population of approximately 309,000. It was established in the 1930s when five villas were built; two additional villas were provided in 1953, two in 1967 and two in 1971.

We rented from the Hospital Board a detached house standing in about an acre of land, and separated from the hospital by a side-road leading to the main entrance and a farm. The house at one time had been a pub, i.e., several centuries before, and the basement had a floor which in part had flagstones, and in the other part was bare earth. One of the sections had a well which fortunately was covered securely, and the other had a stone oven for baking bread; this area had been used as a kitchen for the pub. The attic was floored, and between the basement and attic we had the usual rooms. Just prior to us moving in it had been used as a nurse training school.

Our son, who had started at the local grammar school, was a keen rugby player and was soon involved, spending a lot of his time touring around the countryside and competing in various matches. He also reminded us that we had promised him another dog when his pet poodle had died in Canada. Consequently, we quickly acquired a puppy, a golden Labrador, who initially was able to sleep in a shoebox, but quickly grew to his normal size and bulk, and at the same time became even more boisterous. He was also extremely friendly with other animals. One of our neighbours had a horse and trap, and when our dog was leaning over the garden wall, the horse would stop to pass the time of day with him, much to the annoyance of his master. Similarly, when the cows were being

mustered for milking, each of them had to stop to acknowl-
edge and sometimes rub noses with him, and this caused some
confusion in the ranks, and irritated the farmer.

To complete our "menagerie", we had a Shetland pony,
which was used by the hospital children, and we had agreed
for her to graze in our garden. My wife spoiled her by giving
her titbits, which often led to her entering the house uninvited
if we happened to leave an open door.

The administrative centre for the hospital was in the original manor home of the estate, and my office was in a large
wood-panelled room; it was very imposing. It was there I was
introduced to the senior staff by the Group Secretary of the
Hospital Management Committee, Mr. Reg Dixon. Following
this, I had a tour of the hospital villas, etc., and it was soon
clear that there was an urgent need to make many changes.

My task was facilitated by a report from the Regional Hospital Review Board, which had earlier visited the hospital. The
review body comprised a physician, a director of nursing and
an administrator. They listed the many faults in the
programmes and organisation, and had predicted serious con-
sequences for the future of the institution if major changes
were not made. A time limit was recommended, with the first
critical review to take place six months after my appointment.

My first step was to set up a Professional Advisory Committee with representation from all departments, including the
Group Secretary. The critical report was read in detail and
discussions started on a plan to resolve the problems.

One obvious and immediate concern of mine was the out-
dated complete segregation of the sexes. The hospital was divided into two sections, which resulted in duplication of
programmes and inappropriate use of some of the villas.

For a start, I suggested some rearrangement of programmes
and facilities. There was an immediate rejection or at least
reluctance by many members, but in the end there was agreement to start with a pilot scheme, a villa for older residents

with females in one wing and males in the other wing, but sharing a common room and dining-room. This scheme was a great success, with the older men improving their manners and behaviour, and the ladies appreciating the attention. It provided the impetus and improved staff confidence to move forward.

Soon after, I was astonished to be met in my office by my predecessor who was apparently shocked at seeing residents holding hands and occasionally kissing, and accused me of promoting promiscuity among the residents. I reminded him that during his administration there were a number of illegitimate births and love affairs, and assured him that the new programmes would probably reduce the birth rate as the sexes could meet openly and there was no need to hide in the surrounding trees when having an illicit affair.

Time out from the hospital was also previously arranged around the sex of the resident, with weekend leave based on one weekend for males and so on. On the first weekend when residents were preparing to go into town, I was surprised to see some of the ladies and the men crying. When questioned, they said they were very concerned about people's reaction to them being in town together.

No untoward event followed this relaxation; in fact, within a short time the older members formed their own club and participated fully with other senior clubs in the community. They staged a very sucessful party for their associates at the hospital.

Another innovation was the regular Saturday-night dance in the recreation hall. This was a tremendous success, but on at least one occasion an embarrassment to me. I had decided to pay a visit to the dance, and when I was invited to participate there were hoots of laughter and amusement when the residents discovered "the Boss" couldn't perform the "Slosh" dance.

During these changes I became very interested in Charlie.

He was a man in his fifties who started to play a leading role in the "Over 60s Club". He acted with confidence and control as M.C. at the invitational party for the guest clubs, and helped to organise many of the club activities. He was also my gardener, and took great pride in his work. On reviewing his case file, I could find little reason for his stay in the hospital. He had been admitted to an institution as a teenager for theft, and was said to be mentally handicapped. Later he had been discharged but started thieving again, and was admitted to the hospital.

When questioned, he stated that if he was released to the community he might start stealing again, but it wasn't clear why he had started in the first place.

After some further discussions and review, we were able to find work for him in the Parks Department at Maryport, and arranged for him to continue living in the hospital and to travel each day to work. This continued for several months until he regained his confidence, and eventually he found an apartment and was discharged. When I had moved back to Canada, he wrote to me to inform me of his marriage and continued success at work.

The two units built in 1971 for children were a blight on the hospital. As a consequence of the policy of segregating the sexes, one unit was for females and the other for males. In practice this created an impossible situation. Staff had to care for severely physically and mentally handicapped children while at the same time cope with hyperactive children bent on mischief. The interior of the buildings looked like a war zone with holes in the walls, fixtures pulled from the walls, and furniture in a state of disrepair or broken.

It was therefore no surprise to find the Board of Management unwilling to spend more money repairing the damage. The plan was to use one residence for severely handicapped children of both sexes, and the other as a behavioural unit. In addition, the Board was asked to ignore Regional Hospital Board practice of bulk buying, and allow the children in the

behavioural unit to be involved in the planning and local purchase of furnishings. In this way, it was contended, the children would have some pride in their choice, and would not
destroy the things that they had personally chosen. With the
concentration of behavioural problems in the one unit, it would
also be possible to introduce a behavioural programme with
incentives to counter the previous unstructured approach.

After some considerable debate, the Board agreed that they
did not have much choice, as the current conditions were un-
tenable. And so with some trepidation we started implement-
ing the plan.

In planning and preparing programmes for the severely
handicapped children, we brought in Mildred Stevens, a special education expert from Cheshire. I had previously met
Mildred when she was in Fredericton, New Brunswick as a
visiting consultant to the Education Department, and in addition to her help in planning, she provided some in-service
training for staff.

Considerable help was also provided by our blind physiotherapist. John Sealby was a remarkable man; blindness did
not appear to be a major problem to him, as he was able to
move freely throughout the hospital, and he was a very frequent passenger on buses. He was very sensitive to the difficulties of communication with severely mentally handicapped
children, and helped overcome many of these problems with
sensory and physical stimulation as well as by behavioural
modification techniques. His services were also in great demand in the community, and he helped many families with
his advice and treatment. It was an inspiration to work with
him, and to see the changes in the children's development,
associated behaviour and responses.

One major problem was the lack of an experienced psychologist on the staff. There was a considerable shortage of
psychologists in the area, but we did manage to get some help
from the educational psychologists who, nevertheless, had very

limited experience in developing institutional programmes, nor did they have much time to spare. A promise of money for a senior psychologist was obtained from the hospital board. Meanwhile, with the enthusiastic help of staff and the children, the programme got off to a good start and there was a marked drop in destructive behaviour. In fact, the children and staff had mutual enjoyment in actively participating in the planning and selection of furnishing and decorating of the new unit.

We also set up a behavioural unit for adults, but without a psychologist, this proved to be a difficult task. As best we could, we tried different approaches but with limited success. One programme involved patients making the rules and deciding appropriate punishment, but staff were reluctant to give up their authority and control.

One lady, who was buxom and strong, created many problems by her aggressive behaviour. She enjoyed sitting on the wall overlooking the main highway and calling abuse at passing motorists or throwing stones. Fortunately, we were able to persuade her to more constructive activities. On another occasion she locked herself in the washroom and refused to come out. I was called, and after I had talked to her for several minutes, she pulled the W.C. from its fittings and used it to smash the door down. After that she stood glowering and threatened to throw the sanitary convenience at me, but eventually we were able to calm her and persuade her not to engage in the damaging action she initially had in mind.

With a careful screening and help from the Social Service Departments, we were able in a relatively short period of time to reduce the number of beds from 400 to 360. In spite of this, we still had some overcrowding and managed to obtain the promise of a new 30-bed unit and a new hostel in the community.

While our reorganization was proceeding, we received a few visits from the Hospital Review Board. I found these visits rewarding as we were able to discuss the progress constructively and it was possible to get some good feedback as well as helpful suggestions. It was also reassuring to have positive reports from the Board, and it helped staff morale when their findings were circulated.

In the community, meetings were held with national and local voluntary associations, and Local Authority Departments. An appointment by the Regional Hospital Board to an Advisory Committee on the implications of the Gray Paper on "Management Arrangements for the Reorganized National Health Service", was appreciated. Among other things, the government proposed the establishment of Area Health Authorities accountable to Regional Health Authorities. The committee was composed of senior physicians from the various branches of medicine, and was conducted in a very formal manner. My Canadian experience caused me to upset some of the more staid members of the committee. One afternoon in the summer, when the hot sunlight was radiating through the windows, and we all sat perspiring in our best suits, I did what was normal in Canadian circles; I rose from my chair, took my jacket off and placed it over the back of the chair, loosened my tie and collar, and sat down again. There was complete silence; then after several seconds the chairman addressed me, while a few members appeared to regard me with disdain:

"Dr. Short, we will resume the meeting when you are properly dressed."

"Mr. Chairman, I'm sorry to disagree with you. I am the only one who is now properly dressed. It is very uncomfortable and absurd in this heat to be wearing a jacket and to be sweating so much."

"We will resume the meeting when you are properly dressed."

The jacket had to be put back on a hot and sweaty body, and collar and tie repositioned so that we could resume our cooler deliberations.

At another meeting when a member made a statement which I considered to be fatuous, and in keeping with the relaxed and frank level of Canadian discourse, I bluntly expressed my opinion. This upset the honourable member, and the chairman instructed me to address my remarks through the chair in a more courteous manner. In reply, I stated through the chair that "Unless the member's statement could be verified by facts, I maintain my opinion."

In spite of my rebellious ways, it was a surprise when I was appointed to the Regional Medical Advisory Committee, which succeeded the above Advisory Committee.

During the machinations of government reorganization, I was privileged to have a meeting with the Minister for the Department of Health and Social Security. We met in September 1973 and I was asked to document my thoughts in a letter. My concern was that the reorganization of the Health Service could lead to further estrangements between health and social services. My particular anxiety was for the services for the mentally handicapped, and I pressed for a phased approach with joint and meaningful planning between hospital service and local authorities.

The Minister was very sincere and interested in my views and appeared genuinely anxious to avoid the pitfalls which change, and the accompanying insecurity, could provoke. In his written reply, he confirmed these sentiments.

While I was involved in administrative and service changes, my wife and I were facing another change. Our daughter was teaching in Edinburgh and had changed her recreation from parachute jumping to exploring the deep caverns and passages within the earth – in other words she was pot-holing. While participating in this pastime she met her future husband.

Peter didn't exactly endear himself to me, especially on his first visit. He had brought our daughter, Aileen, to our home and after a late supper drove off for Liverpool.

We retired to bed, then about 1 a.m. our sleep was interrupted by a telephone call to request my help. He had run out of petrol and was stranded on the highway about 30 miles from our home. Consequently I had to collect him and take him back in the morning with some fuel for his vehicle.

Not long after this episode, they announced their intention to get married. They wanted to set the date for sometime in April, which did not allow much time to arrange a wedding. We managed to persuade them to postpone the wedding until October. It had to be a quiet affair, but by the time the wedding guest list had been completed, it had grown so much that we had to book a hotel, etc.

The wedding went off without a hitch, but it was a very exhausting weekend. The arrangements were for the wedding ceremony to be at noon on the Saturday, and festivities finished by 4 p.m. so that the guests could get back home to Liverpool or Edinburgh and Glasgow. However, the best-laid plans of mice and men gang aft agley! Guests started arriving on the Thursday, and the pot-holing group arrived on the Friday, complete with camping gear, but they finished up in the attic. Other friends arrived with their caravan and parked it at the side of the house. Everyone else had booked into local hotels from Friday to Sunday. On the Friday evening we had over two dozen people in the house, and few retired before 2 a.m. Fortunately we had discovered, just prior to the event, the intention of our guests to have a prolonged celebration, and we had to quickly organise a second reception and dance in the recreation hall of the hospital. This had to be over by midnight, but about 30 guests came back to our house and continued the festivities until about 3 a.m.

Later that Sunday morning when we greeted our friends, we found that the pot-holing club had taken over our kitchen and meals were prepared and served by them. Indeed, we were not allowed to take any responsibility for the rest of Sunday and when the last of the guests left that night, dishes were washed and everything was in order.

About two weeks before the wedding I had been at the Hague, Holland, to attend an international conference on mental retardation. At this conference I met a good friend, Dr. Allan Roeher, Executive Vice-President of the Canadian Association for the Mentally Retarded and Founding Director of the National Institute on Mental Retardation at York University, Toronto. We had worked together on a number of issues, and he had been very annoyed at me for leaving Canada. When we were parting, Allan said, "You must come back to Canada." My reply was, "I'll think about it if you find me something which will interest me and not be tainted by political intrigue."

Several weeks later, just after the wedding, I received a phone call from Edmonton, Alberta, inviting me to the province for a week to view the services and discuss the option of employment as Associate Director of Services for the Handicapped.

Regrettably this offer had to be put on hold because of an event which caused us much anguish, and caused me to have some misgivings about some of my colleagues. Towards the end of November 1973, just over a month after our daughter's wedding, she suffered an illness which her doctor thought was influenza. However, we began to be concerned when she refused to speak to us on the telephone. This was completely out of character for her, and we asked her husband to take her back to her doctor.

After seeing her doctor, they were not happy with his assessment of her condition and arrived unexpectedly at our home. She was very restless, irritable and aggressive; in fact, her behaviour was quite bizarre.

At first I suspected that she was in a manic phase of depression and wondered if she was having side effects from "the pill". Following a few days of observation I decided that she might be suffering from encephalitis, an infection which affects the brain cells. She had severe sleep disturbance, wandering about the house at night, had poor concentration and intermittent blurring of her vision. On physical examination, I could find no definite clinical signs. Our local family physician was called in and he confirmed my suspicions. We then arranged for her admission to the General Hospital.

Further tests failed to confirm the diagnosis, although there was a slightly abnormal rise in the number of lymphocytes in her cerebro-spinal fluid.

By the middle of December she had deteriorated further, and I was surprised and concerned when she was transferred to the psychiatric unit. My concerns were discussed with the psychiatrist, who nevertheless was adamant in his diagnosis of severe depression, and refused to consider any other cause. Ultimately I agreed to her receiving anti-depressant medication, but her condition continued to worsen, and she gradually lapsed into a semi-comatose state.

When the medication was not producing positive results, the psychiatrist recommended electro-convulsive therapy (commonly known as electric shock treatment). I was furious, and warned her husband not to sign any consent form without my knowledge or approval. In addition, the psychiatrist was warned that he would face litigation if he proceeded with his plan.

At this time I began to question if I was acting as an over-protective parent, and allowing this to cloud my professional judgement. To test this I telephoned my good friend and mentor, Dr. Jim Affleck in Edinburgh. I told him that I had a serious disagreement with our local psychiatrist over a patient's diagnosis and sought his views. Thereupon I detailed the symptomatology and clinical and laboratory test results; after some more questioning, he supported my point of view and it was then he was told the patient was my daughter.

With this reassurance, I immediately contacted a neurologist who was visiting the hospital, and after I explained to him the controversy over the diagnosis, he agreed to examine Aileen. His provisional diagnosis was viral encephalitis, and he recommended treatment back in the medical unit.

Over Christmas and New Year, we sat at Aileen's bedside watching her lapse into coma, until in desperation I telephoned the neurologist in Newcastle and arranged for her admission to the intensive care unit, Royal Victoria Infirmary, Newcastle. On admission, the neurologist was uncertain our daughter would survive; she had a tracheotomy, and was linked to life support systems.

Fortunately she did survive and began to improve. More tests were carried out. Then I received a call from the neurologist. He had good news and bad news. The cause of her illness had been found: it was due to Cryptococcus Neoformans, a fungus. The bad news was that the illness was extremely serious and often fatal; at that time there was only one drug on the market which provided any hope, but unfortunately it had serious side-effects.

When I checked with my textbooks, one published in 1951, it stated: "Spontaneous cure is almost unknown and most cases die in 4-8 weeks from the onset; those who survive an acute attack drag on for a few months or years to a fatal ending with coma and respiratory failure." Another textbook, published in 1965, described the illness as "a chronic, usually fatal meningitis."

Treatment was started, but she developed serious toxic reactions and within 24 hours the drug had to be stopped.

At this stage we were faced with a dilemma. Should we start to consider withdrawing the life support, or should we continue in the hope of at least a partial recovery? If she makes a recovery, could she be so severely brain-damaged that she would have a vegetative existence?

While these thoughts were being considered, my wife was staying with our close friends, the Robertsons; and I was driving back and forth between Cockermouth and Newcastle. Each weekend her husband, Peter, was driving over 70 miles from Dunfermline to be with her.

The next developments slowly changed our despair to hope-fulness. The neurologist phoned to ask permission to try a drug, which was having clinical trials in the hospital and had been found to be effective against some fungal diseases. The drug was called Flucytosine.

As we had nothing to lose, we agreed. Meanwhile my wife was advised to sit at Aileen's bedside and to keep trying to communicate with her in the hope of getting some response. After several days on the new medication and no sign of im-provement, the question of discontinuing the life support came up again. This time, driven by despair, my wife shook Aileen and pleaded with her to respond; staff in the unit rushed in when they saw these activities, and all were surprised to see a tear in our daughter's eyes. This convinced the doctors to con-tinue with life supports and their extraordinary efforts.

There were signs of further improvement in the next few days, and the neurologist suggested we should have a break and return home for a short period. As this was at a weekend, we decided to stay in Newcastle overnight, and next day as we were passing the hospital we decided to visit the unit before driving home. To our amazement our daughter had recovered consciousness. In spite of the fact that she had no voice, she was able to indicate that she wanted her mother to stay.

Aileen continued to make good progress and started com-municating by writing on paper. She also started crocheting, and asked her mum to get presents for some of her friends who were having babies. From then on her recovery could only be described as miraculous – indeed an answer to prayer. She was back teaching by September with no evidence of neu-rological damage, although she had a very strict follow-up period of treatment and testing for a year.

While we waited in anguish for the survival of our daugh-ter, Marcel Arcand, the Director of Services for the Handi-capped, Alberta, had kept in touch with us, and with her re-covery we had to start thinking of our future. We discussed the possibility of returning to Canada with our daughter and son-in-law; they insisted that we seriously consider this, and promised that they would emigrate as soon as they could if we decided to make the move.

Consequently, towards the end of March 1974, I accepted the offer to visit Alberta for a week to discuss an appointment and to view the services. I stayed with my old boss from New Brunswick, Dr. Graham Clarkson, and had a very enjoyable and interesting visit.

Soon after my arrival in Edmonton I met with Marcel and the Minister, Neil Crawford. We had a stimulating discussion about the expectations of the department, and the responsibilities of the proposed appointment.

Following this meeting I was provided with an extensive tour of services in the province, and was also brought face to face with the hard winter conditions which could prevail at this time, and the associated travelling hazards.

Graham's wife, June, drove me to the airport one day when I was flying for a visit to services in Calgary. We had to drive through a blizzard, and I just had time to get my ticket, and was last on board the aircraft. No sooner had I buckled up when the pilot welcomed us aboard, then announced that he couldn't see much from his viewpoint because of the snow, but we would taxi to the end of the runway and hope for the best. Within minutes we were airborne. Later, I had to bundle into a Twin Otter airplane, again in a blizzard, to fly to Red Deer.

The visit was extremely informative, and I received assurances from the Minister that the political situation in Alberta was different from the Maritimes.

Soon after my return home we started our preparations for a move to Canada, and this set in motion a few more problems.

We had purchased a building lot in Cockermouth, and our new home was almost complete. However, the biggest headache was the Canadian Immigration Department.

When we initially applied to emigrate to New Brunswick, the process was very simple. We travelled to the Canadian Office in Glasgow, had our medical, completed some forms and had an interview. Our documents were received a few days later.

This time, in April 1974, we had to apply to the London Office, and as soon as we received the application forms we had our medical examination and I mailed the results back to London.

Several weeks elapsed with no communication. I therefore telephoned the department and talked to a very officious bureaucrat who first denied that he had received our application and our medical report. When informed that I had mailed all of the relevant documents several weeks previously and that they had been sent by registered mail, he admitted the documents had been received. When questioned about confirmation of our "landed immigrant status", he harangued me with talk about the number of people applying and refused to give me an estimate when I would receive my documentation. He was reminded that I was due to start working for the Alberta Government in July, but this did not appear to influence him in any way.

More weeks passed, and on the advice of Marcel Aceand, I telephoned Alberta House in London. The officials there were very helpful and promised to apply some pressure.

Still no progress. Once more I telephoned and spoke to the same bureaucrat, who continued to be obstructive.

In the interim we had to make arrangements for moving our belongings and my car. We had decided to take my Ford Galaxie 500 back to Canada, and it was the first to be shipped. I telephoned the intractable official once more, this time informing him we had booked our air flights and that my car was already on the high seas. At this he fumed and ordered me to bring the car back.

As we were now running out of time, I telephoned Alberta House, London, and Edmonton, and within a few days we received our documents. On the day we were moving out we received the key to our new home in Cockermouth, and had to leave the building in the hands of the real estate agent.

So again, we had to bid farewell to friends, to hospital staff and patients as we set out once more overseas, and to another challenge.

CHAPTER 13

THE WANDERER RETURNS

As we approached the Edmonton International Airport on a hot July day in 1974, we could see the highway, which ran north and south from Edmonton to Calgary, the flat prairie wheatlands with patches of spruce trees, small lakes or sloughs, and as we drew near to the airport the adjoining small town of Leduc with the ethereal background of the tall buildings of Edmonton, seen some distance away in the hot haze of summer.

After the customary immigration procedures, we were met by Brian Elliott, the Finance Officer for the Division Services for the Handicapped, who had rented an apartment and furniture for us. Brian was most helpful and took us to the shopping mall to purchase bed linens, towels, etc., which were not available in the apartment. He also proved to be a most competent and innovative member of the central office team.

Our flat was on the 20th floor of a "high-rise" building and we had a panoramic view of the city. However, my wife did not feel relaxed living in a "high-rise". A few days after our arrival we had a visit from Mrs. Brunskill and her daughter. Mrs. Brunskill was a school welfare officer in Whitehaven, England, and she had helped me establish a programme for

"Under Fives". She had married a Canadian pilot and moved to Edmonton at the end of the war. Shortly afterwards he had been killed in a flying accident, and she had returned home to England. This was her first visit back to Edmonton and she was astounded by the changes. It was illuminating for us to listen to her comparison of the city when she had lived in it and now.

We moved into our new home about a month after our arrival and soon found we had a number of enthusiastic Scottish country dancers as neighbours – and they were not all Scottish expatriates. We had never participated in these activities before. As might be expected, we were coerced into joining and within a short period attended a workshop which was very exhausting. The first day we started dancing and practising the steps from 9:30 a.m. to 4:00 p.m. and repeated this the next day, but at the end we had to rush home for a bath and change, then return at 7:00 p.m. for dinner and danced until after midnight. When I was driving home afterwards my legs went into cramp and I had great difficulty and pain in coping with the accelerator and brake pedal.

Unlike my experience in New Brunswick, I was able to register with the College of Physicians and Surgeons, Alberta to practise my profession without restrictions, and signed a contract to be employed as a Consultant in Psychiatry and Mental Retardation and as Associate Director of Services for the Handicapped, a branch of the Department of Health and Social Development. One of the benefits in my contract was paid study leave and money to cover the expenses incurred by attendance at conventions or specific visits or study. This allowed me to visit services in other countries.

The Director of the Branch was Marcel Arcand, a social worker, and in July 1977 he was promoted to Assistant Deputy Minister for the department, and I assumed his position as Director.

In Canada, legislation is provided at federal and provincial levels for health and social services. The federal legislation is designed to provide fiscal support for these programmes, but the planning and implementation are at a provincial level, although attempts are made to ensure some national consistency in the approach to these services. Prior to 1972, the statutory authority for providing services for the mentally handicapped was contained in the Mental Health Act. The provincial government then set up a committee to review the Mental Health Act and to make recommendations. The Blair Report was published in 1969 and in its recommendations on the Mental Health Act, the mentally handicapped were excluded. Instead, by an "Order in Council", the government established a Division of Services for the Handicapped "to ensure adequate services for the mentally and physically handicapped".

In the Throne Speech on March 1972, it was stated;

> "My Government believes there needs to be a much higher priority given to facilities and support for Alberta children who have handicaps and learning disabilities.
>
> "It is felt that Society has a clear obligation to confirm its belief in the equal opportunity concept by providing special help for children who start life with disadvantages. This priority involves not new legislation, but new directions in programs which will be presented for consideration of the members during the course of the session." (Hansard)

The exclusion from the Mental Health Act produced gaps in the legislation and in the ability of services and society to meet effectively some of the problems and needs of the mentally handicapped. To this end the legislature passed the "Dependent Adults Act".

Around this time the Alberta government had conflicting advice. One report (Advisory Services 1972) recommended the building of 400 additional institutional beds in the south of the province, and a similar number to cover the north.

On the other hand, the Blair Report (1969) recommended that the central institution should not be enlarged or duplicated, and that services for the handicapped children should be distributed to the regions.

To add to the government's dilemma, there was considerable pressure for de-institutionalization – and yet this was not without its dangers. In 1975 the "Modern Health Care" published an editorial which stated that:

> *"De-institutionalization was hailed as a grand vision, but the vision has become a nightmare, and the word de-institutionalization has been twisted into a cruel euphemism for dumping hundreds of thousand of sick, dazed people into an unprepared society."*

These remarks were addressed to the U.S. mental health services, but the same situation could apply to the services for the mentally handicapped if this ideal was recklessly introduced.

Another ideology was "normalization", which envisaged all handicapped persons living within a normal environment, and sharing in the same opportunities and comforts that are generally expected within our society. In essence, from dependence to independence through normal channels with a few specialized programmes. Clearly, in many cases much more is needed.

At the same time the politicians in Alberta were abundantly aware of the problems in the community and institutions. When Neil Crawford, Minister of Social Services and Community Health, spoke to the legislature in March 1972, he said:

> *"We were, when we took office, inundated with mail*

and telephone calls from people who were experienc-
ing, in many cases, personal tragedies of their own
directly related to severely handicapped children in
their homes; autistic children, ones who required a
highly specialized degree of care throughout some
period of their young lives, and had not been able to
receive it at all. We were told of a waiting list for
admittance of handicapped children to the Alberta
School hospital in Red Deer that numbered over 600
– 300 of them being classified as emergency cases."
(Hansard)

A few days after my arrival in Edmonton I met the multi-
disciplinary team in the central office. It was a delight to meet
again with Marcel Arcand, the Director of the Division, who
had been so solicitous during our daughter's illness, and with
whom I had corresponded. Brian Elliott was there, together
with Helen Cummings, a nurse and consultant in residential
services; Maria Carey, a psychologist and consultant on child
development services; and last but not least, Dale Joslin, a
social worker and consultant on vocational services.

My responsibility was to assist in developing the growth of
comprehensive community services while reducing the number of residents in the institutions, to reduce the waiting list
and to provide expert consultation and assessment services to
the Director, the institution, and the community agencies.

The implementation of these duties involved a considerable
amount of travelling by car and air. The town of Red Deer,
where the main institution was located, was approximately 90
miles from our base in Edmonton. This meant motoring frequently in severe winter storms, and on one or two occasions,
because of the sub-zero temperatures, the fuel lines froze up
and the car stopped. When this happened one had to sit at the
side of the highway until the heat from the engine melted the
offender. At night we had to plug the car into an electric point

to keep some heat in the engine block, and when there was an extreme drop in temperature the tires would freeze and the section of tire touching the road remained straight causing a bumpy ride until it thawed.

In the southern part of the province we had frequent swings in weather conditions when a "chinook" struck. For example, one day my arrival into Lethbridge was met by a severe snow blizzard, by lunchtime it was raining, and later, on the road back to the airport, we had intense frost and the road conditions were extremely hazardous.

While these conditions might appear grim, there were many compensations. For one thing the houses were all pleasantly warm, with no cold draughts, unlike some of the British homes where heating was often inadequate and at times appeared to be restricted to one area of the room so that there was no overall assimilation of heat by the body. Fortunately, these conditions are improving in these homes.

Social activities were seldom restricted by the inclement weather. We attended many social events when it could have been considered madness to venture out. A good example of this was the Scottish Country Dancing weekends, held in Red Deer on the first weekend following the beginning of the New Year. Many enthusiastic dancers set out, year after year, from various parts of Alberta to assemble for a very energetic and most enjoyable time. The weather was unpredictable; we faced extremely low temperatures, snow blizzards and ice, but somehow we all survived unscathed.

As if weather conditions were not enough, the road configuration in Edmonton sometimes added to the problem. Roads going north and south were streets, while those facing east and west were avenues. This arrangement certainly facilitated finding one's way around town, but problems arose when a street took a bend and became an avenue.

On one occasion, shortly after we arrived in Edmonton, we were invited to the minister's home for a musical evening with several other ministers of the government, Marcel Arcand, and our wives, and with a variety of instruments, including my piano accordion. We anticipated a very pleasant evening and set out early for this social and musical event. Unfortunately, weather conditions were miserable; it was snowing heavily and in the relatively strange surroundings we became completely confused. Adding to our disorientation was the change from street to avenue, and later back to street, only it was a different street from the one on which we had been driving – the one leading to the minister's house. Thus we arrived late, apologetic and abashed.

Nor did the sub-zero temperatures deter our outdoor activities. Provided there were mild wind conditions and it was sunny, and these conditions frequently prevailed, we were able to go for walks or cross-country ski. It was very stimulating to ski for miles on the frozen Saskatchewan River and to end up congregating around a fire, roasting wieners on a stick and drinking hot chocolate or coffee, which we brought in flasks. My family and friends were very amused on one occasion when I formed the rearguard, and after labouring and sweating up a hill with my skis, and just before I reached the brim, I stopped and waved. In doing so, I brought my skis round so that they no longer acted as a brake and I started moving backwards at an increasing speed; this required considerable skill which I did not have! After my ignominious retreat I had to retrace my tracks, but this time I carried my skis.

Another complication was the indeterminate working hours. Civil servants are frequently thought to be in a sinecure with regular hours, and Ministers of the Crown too busy playing politics with little time for the constituents. It certainly was not like that in our case. Ministers worked for long hours and, as senior officials, we were expected to be on call during the day or in the evening when ministers met with members of the public, groups of concerned citizens or those with vested interests. One minister had the deplorable habit of announcing, usually in the late afternoon of a Friday, that he was leaving on a weekend tour of his rural area and I was expected to meet him at the airport in two or three hours. This sometimes led to difficulty in keeping awake, especially when the meeting stretched on beyond midnight. In this befuddled state it was not always possible to keep alert for questions referred by the minister or by a committee member. It was also necessary to keep a bag packed, and my wife had to suffer changed plans for supper or weekend activities.

Aside from the hazards associated with the weather and travel, I had to adjust again to the less formal Canadian approach. There was a quick reminder when, a few weeks after my arrival in Alberta, a request was received for my participation at a conference organised by the Alberta Rehabilitation Council for the Disabled. It was held in a holiday camp just outside of Edmonton, and the audience was dressed informally – in jeans and T-shirts. I had reverted to British formality, and dressed in my best suit, shirt and tie, and sweating in the summer heat, addressed the participants. Shortly after the start of my address a voice from the back shouted, "Take off your jacket", a few minutes later, "Take off your tie" – quite the reverse of my English experience.

The challenge for the provincial government and, of course, the Division, was the large institution in Red Deer with its 2400 residents who had a wide range of mental and physical handicaps; about 400 were over the age of 60. Then there was the waiting list of 600 children and over 300 adults.

In Calgary, about 180 miles from Edmonton, was the Baker Centre, an old sanatorium previously used for cases of tuberculosis; it was now used to house 145 severely handicapped children.

How do you reduce the number of residents in the institutions, and at the same time diminish the waiting list? Why were they admitted to the institution in the first place?

The answer to the last question is that there are many reasons. Doctors and friends may have urged this step because it would be easier on the family, the handicapped child could be perceived as an embarrassment or could potentially interfere with employment opportunities, and so on. On the other hand, parents could blame one another for the defect – "We have nothing like this in **our** family," or they simply may feel guilty, fearing they may have done something wrong. The stress on a marriage can be profound.

Putting aside the emotional stress, there is a severe physical strain, usually on the mother, especially when the handicapped child suffers from associated physical handicaps or distressing epilepsy.

Once admitted to an institution, a number of parents may start with regular visits and gradually reduce the number of visits until the child or adult is forgotten. Conversely, a number of parents or relatives faithfully assume a ritual of regular visits and occasionally take the resident back home for a day or more. Nevertheless, the institution, with the other handicapped persons, comprised the major environment.

What are the handicaps? They are myriad. Some children can read and write a little, many cannot. Some can carry out self-care skills, some cannot; but many can be trained to live a relatively normal life if given the environment and the required support. Those in the community have a good chance to remain there if they and the family get help and support they need.

An example of successful return to the community, which also illustrates the need for support to face the challenge, can be seen in the account published in "The History of Michener Centre 1923-1983". Doreen was admitted to the institution when she was seven, and spent 15 year of her life there until 1946 when she was discharged to work on a farm. In this kind of work she was still relatively isolated, and in 1960 she was re-admitted. Later she had day jobs when she would return to the institution at nights. She was discharged to a group home in 1976, and shortly afterwards she moved into an apartment. She stated: "I like living on my own, but I still have the group home to fall back on if I run into any problems. Without that I wouldn't have felt as I do."

At the other extreme is the severely handicapped person, sometimes with multiple problems, exemplified by the child suffering from hydrocephalus; this is a congenital condition with blockage in the circulation of the fluid within the skull, resulting in an enlargement of the cranium and a vegetative existence. To-day many of these cases can be avoided by implanting a mechanical device or shunt, but a number remain.

Even when there are no such complications, the poor intellect and deficient level of functioning precludes independent living, and these incompetences can be compounded by life in an institution or a home where over-protective parents isolate the child, or when they do not receive the help that is needed.

One such case concerned a boy who was reared by his parents from infancy until he was 40 years old. As a result, both parents lived a very restricted life with few social contacts because of the enormous burden he imposed, his incontinence, his bizarre behaviour, and as he matured in years, he was seen by neighbours and others as a sexual menace, in spite of the fact that there were no grounds for this supposition. There was no relief from community services. When the mother died, the father and daughter struggled on until the daughter married, when there was no recourse but to admit him to an institution.

Another problem is the handicapped person with a behavioural problem. One case that comes to mind was a young attractive girl who was able to function quite well; alas, her behaviour restricted her independence. She had been banned from special school, and when she reached puberty her behaviour deteriorated further, her parents were exhausted, they faced abuse from the neighbours, and in the end she was admitted.

Returning to the first question about reducing numbers in the institution and waiting lists, when the Division was established it was given clear instructions to develop an immediate programme whereby 200 beds would be made available in the year 1972, some in Edmonton, a few extra in the institution and the remainder in group homes in various communities in the province.

The long-term objectives were to review the waiting list of 600 children and to explore other alternatives as to their placement. It was also proposed to conduct a survey of the province "to obtain the necessary information with which to plan the Provincial development of services for these handicapped people".

Thus to meet the immediate needs, new programmes and major renovations were started in the institution, in order to increase the capabilities of the residents and to prepare as many as possible for placement into community facilities.

In Edmonton, an old hospital and nurses' residence, the Cormack Centre, was taken over and renovated and staffed to take 92 severely and multiply handicapped children from the institution in Red Deer.

The Baker Centre, in Calgary, had been operating as an extension of the Red Deer institution for a number of years; the responsibility for its administration was transferred to the Regional Co-ordinator of the Division. The primary role had been the accommodation of 145 severely handicapped children. In the latter part of 1973 the cabinet approved renovations and additional facilities for the Baker Centre site, and the plan to transfer 50 mentally handicapped children and adults from the Red Deer institution back to their home community in Calgary.

Between Edmonton and Red Deer at Wetaskiwin, a small institution for 40 severely mentally handicapped children was under contract to the Child Welfare Branch. This facility was purchased by the government and assigned to Services for the Handicapped in the spring of 1974.

At the same time, during the start-up year, grants were extended to 26 local agencies to establish and operate sheltered workshops, community residences and child development programmes for the handicapped. Over $1,300,000 was granted for the development of new or expanded facilities.

The Division of Services for the Handicapped adopted six regional geographic areas within the province for the development of regional programmes. Regional staff were responsible for ensuring that the handicapped obtained the necessary services at the community level whenever possible, and that the community agencies received assistance in determining local needs and establishing required services. They were also given responsibility for institutional admissions, and for the placement of mentally handicapped persons from their institution back into the community.

One of my first tasks was to become more familiar with the provincial services and staff. The institution at Red Deer was known as the Alberta School Hospital/Deerhome, and later renamed "The Michener Centre" after Roland Michener, who was the Governor General of Canada and who had grown up in Lacombe, near Red Deer.

The institution started in 1923 in a building which had previously been a ladies' college. In its first full year of operation it admitted a total of 108 residents, and by 1972 the population had grown to approximately 2400 with a large waiting list. About 900 of the residents were children and the remaining 1500 were adults. Many of the residents had lost all connection with their parents or relatives. Even where relatives were alive and in touch with the handicapped resident, their experience had sometimes been so traumatic that they were apprehensive or unwilling to risk further stress.

Another major problem was overcrowding, with the result that 40 to 60 persons were herded into large dormitories, there was rapid staff rotation, insecurity, and poor learning experience.

The obvious solution to overcrowding was to discharge residents to the community and demolish buildings. But this meant that alternative community residences must be available, that support services such as workshops, social centres, etc., must be provided, and the number of handicapped discharged must be limited to the level of public acceptance within the province. To inundate a community which is unwilling or ill-prepared for these residents could be traumatic to both parties.

To plan and develop services takes time and dollars; to prepare the handicapped for this venture takes a change in environment, training, and staff re-orientation.

A start had been made with renovations and refurnishing; brighter colours were introduced and terrazzo floors replaced with carpets.

Later a large field on the southern edge of the institution grounds, owned by the institution, was opened up for expansion of the city's Michener Hill subdivision; this subdivision included 21 family homes which were used as group homes. Thus the physical and psychological boundaries and barriers between the institution and the city residential area were dissolved in the process.

In addition, a new multi-use recreation complex was built for the use of the general public as well as residents of the institution. This was opened in March 1977.

No problems were experienced in selling the homes in the subdivision, and this experiment worked very smoothly. It should be noted, however, that the group homes in the subdivision were staffed by experienced staff, and any resident who did present a problem could easily be re-admitted to the institution. In addition a psychologist, physiotherapist and social worker were added to the staff.

Consequently, during all the changes within the institution and the discharge of higher-functioning residents, Michener

Centre gradually offered more specialised services for the severely or profoundly handicapped, and in 1978 we opened a Behavioural Training Unit; this service was expanded in 1980/81 and more sophisticated behavioural programmes introduced.

It was recognised that our planning of services should include the emotional and behavioural problems of the increasing number of mentally handicapped persons in the community. We anticipated a possible increase in pressure for admission to mental hospitals and other institutions; mounting pressure on the police and penal system for inappropriate placements; and finally the effect on public opinion, which was more tolerant than supportive, becoming incensed and once more intolerant.

The problem included the residents from the institution who needed to be integrated back to the community and the mentally handicapped person who required services to prevent his or her admission. For the institutional resident, the transition and prevention of behavioural problems can be facilitated when the resident has had regular exposure to the community and has had adequate preparation for the change. Where custodial care and isolation prevail, the re-orientation is formidable and stressful, and more likely to create serious behavioural problems.

Similarly at home, where the handicapped person is sheltered and encouraged to become submissive and helpless, any rapid change in circumstances which enforce the need for more independence can lead to trauma and problems.

Persons suffering from mental handicap can also develop mental illness like any other individual, and it is essential that staff caring for these persons in the institution or community should be able to differentiate between those symptoms which can be termed "psychiatric" and those due to other causes.

Consequently in 1977, we developed guidelines for the development of services for behavioural and emotionally disturbed mentally handicapped persons.

There is no doubt, especially in institutions, that some of the behavioural problems are directly instigated by or are the inadvertent result of staff attitudes and actions. It is also true that caring for and attempting to habilitate mentally handicapped persons with persistent behavioural problems can be hazardous, emotionally draining, and at times extremely frustrating. For these reasons it is imperative that a system of mechanisms are developed which help maintain morale and, associated with this, the skills and competence of the staff.

While professional associations were expected to ensure a "Code of Ethics", it was felt that the policy of the department was to complement these codes by providing direction and a mechanism to protect the rights of the individual receiving care and treatment, and to ensure that there was adequate documentation and monitoring mechanisms in place.

Later, in July 1978, I was fortunate to be able to visit Denmark and Sweden to study their legislation and their methods and programmes for the mentally retarded exhibiting behavioural problems. It had been 10 years since my last visit to Denmark, so that I was able to make some comparisons.

During my visit I found considerable concern about proposed changes in Danish legislation, which would result in fewer persons being diagnosed and treated as mentally handicapped. As a consequence it was anticipated that more of the handicapped would be sentenced to prison. The proposed changes also included a change from state to county responsibility. It was contended that the national direction would suffer, with counties differing considerably in their interest and commitment. One reason suggested for the change was the escalating costs resulting in an attempt by the national government to spread the financial responsibility. This sounds familiar even to-day.

Of special interest, and in contrast to the North American scene, the Danes and Swedes were reluctant to use intensive

behaviour modification programmes because of the potential dangers of excess or abuse by staff – both countries favoured music therapy and intensive physical recreation, with some psychotherapy.

Just prior to this visit I had to make another transatlantic crossing, on this occasion to cope with a family emergency. In April 1978, my brother and his wife were killed by a drunk driver. This tragic incident was the third time we had to bury two spouses together. My maternal grandfather had died of a heart attack and next day my grandmother died in her sleep; my father suffered from a cerebral thrombosis but was making a good recovery when my mother was killed on her way to the hospital; seven hours later my father died. Thus three generations suffered similar fates.

Continuing on this personal note, we were able to sponsor our daughter and son-in-law, and were happy to welcome them to Alberta, Canada in 1977. Our daughter's qualifications for teaching were not acceptable within the province without more study and examinations. Consequently she decided to enter the banking system, and made a successful career in this field.

Peter, whose expertise was in computers, initially had great difficulty in finding employment in his area of interest, and had to temporise by working as a salesman for electrical components for a short period. Much to our surprise he was very successful as a salesman, but fortunately after a relatively short period he obtained employment in his speciality.

Then in May 1981 our son, Iain, was married and just over a year later we were presented with our first grandchild, Stephanie. Needless to say, we were very happy with these events, and also later when our family grew by two grandsons, Daniel and Patrick.

To add to our joy, Aileen produced a daughter, Nicola, in July 1988. When we learned of our daughter's pregnancy I was very concerned about the possibility of genetic damage caused by the very potent medication she had received during her life-threatening illness. I suggested she should have amniocentesis to determine if such a risk existed, but she refused because of the slight risk of abortion caused by the procedure. In any case, she was determined to have the baby at any price. Fortunately, the baby was bright and healthy, and we have been fortunate to enjoy our grandchildren, even though we are now separated from them by distance.

Turning back to the problems of service delivery, Blair in his report stressed the need to concentrate on problems and personnel, and less on buildings. Therefore the improvement of staff competencies and career opportunities also occupied our attention. Following discussion with the Department of Further Education, we established "Rehabilitation Practitioner Courses" in the colleges based on the National Course and standards developed by the National Institute on Mental Retardation. Under this plan, four levels of training were proposed, ranging from a certificate course to university graduate course. The nurses' course in the institution was terminated.

Another problem was the widening variety of professionals and volunteers in the service. The Canadian Commission on Emotional and Learning Disorders in Children (The Celdic Report 1969) when reviewing staffing and manpower problems stated:

> "Our field visits have convinced us that some of
> these problems are inherent in the way that profes-
> sionals are educated; in the way that staff services are
> organised and in the reluctance to use persons with
> different training and capable volunteers as part of
> the caring team."

Clearly, separate training programmes contribute to many of the interprofessional rivalries and struggles for status. An approach was therefore made to the Department of Further

Education, and later the University of Calgary introduced the first co-ordinated multi-disciplinary series of courses in the area of rehabilitation concerned with mental handicap and allied disorders. Courses were offered at undergraduate and graduate levels, and to other students registered for degrees in other faculties through the use of options within their programmes of study.

Examination and competency results therefore reflect on the ability and awareness of teachers, students, service employers and handicapped persons to define and clearly describe the various ingredients of professional and service needs and solutions.

Sir Winston Churchill wrote an apt description of the dilemma. He described it as follows:

> *"These examinations were a great trial to me, the subjects which were dearest to the examiners were almost invariably those I fancied least. I would have liked to be examined on history, poetry and writing essays. The examiners on the other hand were partial to Latin and Mathematics, and their will prevailed.*
>
> *Moreover, the questions which they asked on both these subjects were almost invariably those to which I was unable to suggest a satisfactory answer. I should have liked to have been asked to say what I knew. They always tried to ask me what I did not know. When I would have willingly displayed my knowledge, they sought to expose my ignorance. This sort of treatment had only one result, I did not do well in examinations."*

At a provincial level we organized a committee to bring together the various interests in order to advise on curricula as well as service needs, and at a national level the N.I.M.R. set up a Committee on Mental Retardation Manpower. As a result of these developments, a mechanism was established to allow national accreditation of the training, thus providing a major advantage over the old mental deficiency nursing qualification, which was not recognised outside of the training institution.

Another area of concern was the needs of severe and profoundly handicapped children. When I visited the Baker Centre in Calgary, I was perturbed by the number of children with gross developmental defects and by the wide variety of clinical conditions. While the staff worked valiantly with these children, they received no support or help from paediatricians. Consequently, an approach was made to the university, and we were very fortunate to obtain the services of Dr. Robert Haslam, Professor of Paediatrics, University of Calgary, and Chairman of the Canadian National Council on Prevention. Dr. Haslam and his staff proved to be a tremendous resource and support to Baker Centre staff and to the regional services; they gave advice and help, not only in clinical services, but also in the planning and development of community support services.

Dr. Haslam also chaired a Symposium on Primary Prevention of Handicapping Conditions, which was sponsored jointly by the Centre for the Study of Mental Retardation, the University of Alberta, and Alberta Social Services and Community Health.

In the 1973/74 budget, funds were provided for 155 spaces for specialised day training in Edmonton and Calgary. A start was made to explore the existing day care and parent/child development programmes already established under the department's Preventive Social Services Branch, as the basis for integrating day training programmes for mentally handicapped children. By this means it was hoped to reduce the segregation of these children, improve their development and reduce the high cost of specialised programs.

The results of these activities produced a levelling off in

specialised day care and a marked increase in infant development and integrated day care programmes. It should also be noted that these services are relatively inexpensive and cost-effective as they provide a good return in terms of child development, improved parental competencies and attitudes, and reduce the pressure for admission to an institution. As a result of this approach, requests for admission decreased to a trickle compared to the 600 children who were on the waiting list in 1972.

This, of course, raises the question – "How do we judge the success or failure of this new approach? By financial savings?"

It is frequently claimed that community care is less expensive than institutional care, but there are, or were, few studies to substantiate or disprove this hypothesis. In fact, the C.A.M.R. in a study (1968-69) suggested that the cost to provide and develop proper services would be at a prohibitive level.

In Alberta we introduced a programme called the Feasible Placement Approach or Agreement (F.P.A.), which essentially was planned integration of an institution resident, with the associated transfer of institution dollars to help pay for the required community services. As a result of this programme, we transferred, in our first year of operation, 84 residents to the community with $800,000. We had problems convincing the Treasury Board, but when we insisted it had to be the whole scheme or nothing (i.e., no money to general revenue), it was approved.

The impetus for this programme was the concern raised when we realized that both insitution and community costs were spiralling. The budget for the institution had increased at rate far in excess of the inflation rate, the resident population was quickly dropping, and even allowing for urgently needed improvements, it was too high.

Under the guidance of Brian Elliott, a workable formula was developed, and although it was complicated and required considerable co-operation from the staff and community organisations, it proved to be successful. It encouraged a much more efficient organisation, while the regional planning and development of resources for these residents were enhanced. It was also a factor that favourably influenced the politicians when we submitted new requests.

Another measure of success or failure can be in the reduction of beds in the institution and in the results of integration back into the community.

In an attempt to chart a new direction, the C.A.M.R. developed a plan for the seventies to experiment with "more innovative, adaptive, humanizing models of human services delivery". This plan proposed a community services system model, later known under the acronym "Com-serve".

The plan was submitted at the C.A.M.R. convention in Halifax in 1971; I attended, as I was working in New Brunswick at the time, and participated enthusiastically in all the meetings and discussions. I was, therefore, pleased to be involved when the "vision" materialized into "Experimental and Demonstration Projects" (E&D projects), particularly when the first one was established in Lethbridge, Alberta, in 1974.

One of the reasons given for choosing Lethbridge was that Alberta was considered to be behind its neighbouring provinces in the level of community services available to its mentally handicapped citizens. In addition, a tour of the institution in Red Deer by Premier Lougheed and his cabinet in 1971 helped to create a commitment for the development of services at the highest level of political leadership. Yet this political interest assured the establishment of the Division of Services for the Handicapped, and experimentation with community services delivery models in other parts of Alberta over the next few years.

The "E&D project" ran into difficulties right at the start. It leased facilities and services from the local voluntary association, and thereby inherited a deficit of $29,000. Thus the organisers were initially preoccupied with deficit funding and in the maintenance of services; they were unable or restricted in their attempts to address the primary objectives of the project.

Then in a study, agreed to by the parties concerned, the Division of Administrative Policies, Alberta Treasury, reported that the project was reasonably well researched as to determining the needs and indentifying services required, but it was not thoroughly planned out operationally as to the steps required to achieve these services. It took over two years of the project's life before a "Working Agreement" was reached among the E&D committee, the provincial government, and the local voluntary agencies. Similarly, no general research mission for testing the effectiveness of the programme was in place until the middle of the five-year experiment. Moreover, because of its experimental nature, a kind of "fish bowl" psychology developed, not only among personnel involved, but also among other concerned agencies and parents. It was expected to have immediate and simple answers to some complex problems, and the temporary nature or uncertain future of such a project also influenced the confidence of parents and agencies.

The decision to terminate the project at the end of the agreed period was a political one based on the community's response. On December 21, 1979, the minister announced the end of the project, effective March 31, 1980.

Part of the Division's mandate was to develop long-term objectives, and to obtain the necessary information with which to plan the rational development of services for handicapped persons. No written policies or objectives were initially produced, and a rather loose administrative structure evolved which permitted the maximum flexibility at a time when dollar and government commitments were greatest.

However, with the rapid expansion in services, and in accord with the mandate, it was decided early in 1975 that there was a need for a position paper which would document the objectives and policies of the Division, and guide the direction in which services could be developed. Just as we were about to work on the document, an incident occurred which almost prematurely terminated my participation, or indeed my existence.

It was a pleasant sunny spring day as I drove along Kingsway towards the municipal airport to pick up my Regional Director from Calgary. I noted that the road was unusually quiet, and thought how good it was to be alive on such a day. Then it happened.

There was a tremendous crashing sound and my car swerved across the road. When I managed to regain control of the car I looked around for answers. No other vehicles could be seen, the car appeared undamaged – that was until I looked at the rear. The roof at the back of the car was resting on the back seat.

I had been passing a large truck depot that had large floodlights on high standards. A bulldozer had been clearing the yard, had struck the stanchion which obviously had suffered some corrosion, and the whole contraption fell with the large floodlight striking the car. My Ford Galaxy 500 was a two-door coupe, and the lamp had struck the roof just behind the mid-section brace. After the usual investigation I was able to continue on my way to the airport, fortunately to pick up only one passenger, but the sight of my damaged car attracted many curious onlookers.

Needless to say, the police were amazed that I was uninjured, and mystified, assuming the car had been struck by a plane or flying missile, until they saw the remains of the floodlight. Indeed, as they had approached from the front of the car and saw me standing there, they initially thought it was another frivolous call.

I chaired meetings with the central office consultants, with Brian Elliott for Finance and Administration, and a representative from the Research Branch when we met to draft The Paper.

In essence, the general philosophy of the division was to

provide and encourage a comprehensive range of services for the handicapped by the strengthening of existing services to meet the needs, and specialist services to support them, or the provision of specialised programmes not already covered.

Meetings were held with staff from the institution, and with the regional directors and their staff. The institution prepared a summary of residents according to age and ability, and in their preliminary review identified 1008 residents who were regarded as borderline, mildly or moderately retarded. This was in line with other surveys carried out in Canada and elsewhere, suggesting that at least 50 per cent of residents in these institutions did not require this form of care.

At a regional level, the directors and the voluntary agencies had to work with the central office team to identify their objectives over a five-year period which could realistically meet the needs of the mentally handicapped and the physically handicapped in their community, as well as cover their commitment to the institution.

Projections were made for discharges from 1975 to 1985, with detailed implications for programme delivery and staffing needs. The objective was to reduce the population during this period from over 2000 to 925. Any reduction in staff would be met by transfers to community facilities.

By 1978 we had estimated the population in the institution would be 1650; it dropped to 1730. In the community we started with 196 beds and by 1978 we provided 1097 regional residential spaces, compared to our projected figure of 1100 spaces for the mentally handicapped. This did not include the spaces provided in the 22 group homes at Michener Hill subdivision. It is interesting to note that the number of residents in Michener Centre in 1999 was 450.

The priorities were reaffirmed in the position paper and summarized as:

1. Prevention, early child development

programmes and family support;

2. Relief of stresses due to severe physical and/or mental handicap, as well as associated programmes to facilitate and enhance development;
3. Better programmes for behavioural problems, including the forensic aspects.

In addition to the above there was the priority to reduce the size of the Michener Centre in Red Deer. The draft paper which gave details of the proposed "position paper" was circulated in several drafts to senior management of the Department, to the Alberta Association for the Mentally Retarded (A.A.M.R.), and to the Alberta Rehabilitation Council for the Disabled (A.R.C.D.).

While the paper was never formally released as a document for public circulation, it was used by the staff and voluntary agencies as the basis for our growth, and the process of putting together this paper was in itself very useful for starting and focusing discussion on the pertinent issues, which rarely happens between government and the community. In 1976 the Chief Deputy Minister and the Department Management Committee established a goal to develop a long-range (five years) plan for the Department.

Each year we reviewed progress or lack of it, and our projections and objectives with senior staff. One of our regional directors, Perry Kinkaide, coined the words "Growing Together" to describe his resources for the dependent handicapped. It should be noted that we are dependent on one another to provide an effective operation of our services. "Planning Together" includes implementation of these plans, which means "working together", and in the multi-disciplinary process we "grow together".

CHAPTER 14

WORKING TOGETHER

The physically handicapped or physically disabled are terms which represent a collection or fusion of multiple handicaps and disabilities, but no such unification was apparent when the operation and direction of each appendage was examined.

The Alberta scene was not different from the situation in Edinburgh when we started to plan and muster resources. One would have assumed that the Alberta Rehabilitation Council for the Disabled represented the views of all of the associations or societies related to physical disabilities. This was not so.

In March 1975, the Canadian Rehabilitation Council for the Disabled (C.R.C.D.) published its "Five-Year Program Development Study". In this report it stated:

> "Conscious of the disparity of services, fragmentation, lack of co-operation and co-ordination that exists among voluntary health agencies across Canada, C.R.C.D. is committed to a catalyst's role with a view to provide a forum for inter-agency exchange."

When we started to write a position paper, which we hoped could be presented to the government and subsequently used to guide the direction in which services could be developed, we found that the exercise was more difficult than we had assumed.

The collection of factual information created serious obstacles, and definitions were subject to different interpretations in the same way as concepts and philosophies. Deciding needs and priorities therefore was fraught with difficulties.

In order to test our views and facts, we had to discuss these with outside bodies and individuals to ensure their accuracy and acceptability. We wrote to the voluntary associations and received some very useful information, although not all of the associations responded.

When our first draft was circulated, we realised that the paper appeared to devote much more detail to the needs of the mentally handicapped than it did to the physically handicapped. Thus we were not surprised when assertions were made that the development of programmes for the physically disabled was playing second fiddle to programmes for the mentally handicapped.

Of course the reasons for government thrusts in the development of community programmes for the mentally handicapped were primarily due to the fact that at all levels – local, provincial and national – there had been a rigorous assessment of principles, aims and objectives for these services. As a result of this, it had been possible to draw up limited and clearly defined targets, and to set dates for them to be reached. Moreover, there were good national and international statistics which could be reliably used in planning.

The Alberta government in its approach to programme development had also been influenced by the recommendations contained in the Blair Report, as well as by the programmes and targets developed by the Alberta Association for the Mentally Retarded – the sole agency for that group.

Because of the diversity of physical handicaps and confusion over what constituted a handicap or disability, there were no comparative national or international statistics which could comfortably be used in our search for this information. We communicated with the federal departments, with the Canadian Rehabilitation Council for the Disabled, with the libraries and with a number of other organisations.

The Canadian Commission on Emotional and Learning Disorders in Children (1969), after 3 1/2 years of work reported:

> *"The statistics on incidence that we have been able to obtain came from a variety of sources – census surveys, registers, estimates, figures published by schools, service agencies, governments, etc. We have, however, very grave reservations about making comparisons and drawing conclusions from what we have found because of the widely differing definitions and criteria for inclusion on which these incidence statistics are based."*

Our problem was further compounded by the fact that figures relating to the physically handicapped usually include all ages, thus embracing the elderly who included a large proportion of the physically handicapped and whose needs had been partially met through extended health care benefits and pension arrangements.

At the same time the Handicapped Housing Society of Alberta, in its commendable and comprehensive report on the housing needs of the physically handicapped, also experienced this problem – its report stated:

> *"It is difficult to establish the present let alone predict the future need and demand for residential facilities for the handicapped."*

Clearly, there was a need to collect information of sufficient reliability to give planners an opportunity to predict future needs and costs with some degree of confidence. Governments cannot commit funds without assurances and some understanding of future implications.

Apart from the rather mundane view of regarding the handicapped as statistics, there was a need to recognise the diversity of need and to clarify our goals and mutual aspirations. In the initial draft of the position paper we made such an attempt, but it was soon evident from the reaction we received from the various parties to whom we had given copies that there was a need for much more discussion.

We were also aware that there was some resentment against the attempt to produce a government paper, however wellintentioned, without full and open discussion with various interested parties, especially with those who would be affected most, the handicapped and their families.

A major contributor to this decision was the Alberta Rehabilitation Council for the Disabled. We received a 35-page document of constructive criticism of the initial draft.

One immediate result of the feedback was the decision to change the name from "Position Paper", which evidently implied a predetermined decision by the department or government, to "Discussion Paper", which translated the "paper" to a more flexible and more open-minded approach.

Another result of the discussion was the decision to use the Annual Conference of the Alberta Rehabilitation Council as a means to obtain the views of the various associations and the handicapped, and to share the problems we faced, and hopefully to find solutions. This created one amusing incident when I was being introduced at one of these annual conferences. The chairman started by referring to me as a government civil servant; then proceeded to compare me, by implication, with three different kinds of ladies' bras – dictatorship bras, which hold the masses together; Salvation Army bras, which give uplift to the fallen; and civil service bras, which make mountains out of molehills.

We started by taking another look at our information base. It was agreed that a great deal of information was available, but unfortunately much of it was distributed among various associations or government departments. There was also considerable overlap and duplication of information, different criteria were used, and we had few tools which would give us an accurate measurement of the degrees of disability.

The blind and the deaf were perhaps more fortunate in that they had a fairly reliable index to measure the degree of disability.

It was therefore resolved to attempt to pool the information by channelling it through one resource, and by standardising the methods of data collection. However, the mechanism for this had still to be considered.

There was no dispute in the principle of normalization – this envisaged the provision of services and conditions which would allow the handicapped to live a life which is as normal as possible.

Unfortunately, while many pay lip-service to this principle, many obstacles can be raised to frustrate the implementation. The employer can produce an environment which negates the ability of the handicapped to function in that setting; or the handicapped person, because of his anger and frustration, may decide to increase his dependence in order to make others suffer.

One handicapped social worker wrote:

> *"Ever since I contracted polio 18 years ago, and especially since I began to practise clinical social work 11 years ago, I have been trying to understand the emotional impact and varied response to disabling illness or injury. The quality of response seems to bear no relationship to the magnitude of the*

injury or disability. Therefore, I have come to believe
that the physical damage, however devastating, is of
secondary importance as a disabling factor. Of
primary importance is the degree to which the
individual's self-image is shattered and fails to
redevelop as a positive force in the individual's life."

Consequently, an emotionally supportive structure is as important as a prosthesis.

To obtain conditions which will enhance the independence of the handicapped and facilitate integration within normal society requires innovative zeal, resourcefulness and determination; but above all, it requires active participation by the handicapped person in deciding his or her future.

Frequently, special conditions must prevail to accommodate the disability. Sometimes, considerable skill is necessary to integrate the handicapped; it may not be enough to simply find a job or accommodation, or to leave it to the employer – the services must provide the know-how and experience to help the handicapped person and his relatives, landlord or employer to assess the situation, and to make the necessary modifications.

In Edinburgh the Disablement Resettlement Officer of the Ministry of Labour was a tremendous help in assisting the handicapped and employer meet the needs of integration within the work force.

Then the handicapped person may be a complete cripple if he cannot get the equipment he needs to make him mobile. In 1975 in Alberta we had serious gaps in the provision of aids to independent living.

The action group for the disabled were pressing the government to develop a scheme for aids to independent living, which we supported. We warned that as new electronic aids were coming on the market, there was a danger of rapidly escalating costs and the need to adequately assess their effectiveness.

Financial security was another issue which was being considered, and schemes within Canada and in other countries were being reviewed.

I had also been confronted with some of the real financial issues and tragedies which can occur when one is afflicted with a disabling disease.

When I met several members of the Multiple Sclerosis Society in Calgary, the plight of a member was brought to my attention. The man had worked for a considerable number of years for a national company, and as a result of his affliction lost his job and pension. Moreover, because he wanted to continue to work, he was forced to seek employment at a level which provided wages on a par with public assistance. To add to his problems, his marriage broke up and he was left in despair.

If this man had been injured at work, he would have received a pension and could have used this to supplement his earnings. Instead, the diagnosis of the disease "Multiple Sclerosis" meant financial ruin and loss of self-respect. At that time, the provincial government had no plans or programme to provide an assured income for the disabled.

In 1976 a brief was submitted by the A.R.C.D. and the Alberta Action Group for the Disabled to the Minister of Social Services and Community Health. The brief stated that while the government and private agencies were co-operating, there still existed a maze of unco-ordinated services for the physically disabled in the province, and there were also large gaps in the services. It was recommended that there should be an Inter-departmental Co-ordinating Committee at Deputy Minister level.

When replying, the Minister, Miss. H. Hunley, stated that while she concurred with the recommendations, she had concluded that such a committee would be most effective if it were made up of officials at the working levels of programmes, instead of at the Deputy Minister level.

Subsequently I was asked to set up the Committee with representation from eight departments: Advanced Education and Manpower; Education; Housing and Public Works; Labour; Recreation Parks and Wildlife; Transportation; Hospitals and Medical Care; and Social Services and Community Health.

The voluntary agencies were then challenged to establish their own Co-ordinating Committee. The upshot of this challenge was the formation of the CORE Committee to advocate for the physically disabled, and to help determine the needs and possible solutions.

One of the first activities of the Inter-departmental Committee was a study to describe and assess the roles of the various departments in the provision of transportation programmes, and to make recommendations on the changes necessary to reduce overlap and any changes needed in departmental policies to ensure coherence and co-ordinated planning of transportation services for the handicapped.

Experience in Alberta, Ontario, Massachusetts, Edinburgh and elsewhere had shown that considerable progress can be achieved when agencies and government are willing to work together towards a common goal, with mutual trust and respect.

In fact, when there is a crisis it is amazing how quickly barriers are removed and government and community agencies work together. In July 1987, in Edmonton, we suffered from a killer tornado which fatally injured at least 35 Albertans, and there was severe flooding and extensive damage. The Red Cross was helped by many Edmontonians who opened their hearts and homes to victims, and eight or nine hotels offered temporary accommodations, as did schools, and halls owned by churches and voluntary groups. The telephone lines were jammed with callers, and the Alberta Government Telephone Company quickly provided extra lines to the Red Cross.

Firefighters, police, ambulance workers, soldiers, volunteers and despondent relatives sifted through the carnage for survivors; provincial mental health specialists helped victims to cope with the trauma of the storm, and food stores provided sustenance for rescuers and rescued. Finally, a concert was organized, dedicated to the victims of the tornado and to provide a relief fund.

When this occurred, I was working in the Rehabilitation Centre and our first recognition that something was up was the intensity of darkness and later a hail-storm, with hail as big as golf balls, which damaged roofs and cars. My wife saved some of them to show me when I got home. Just minutes before the tornado struck she had decided to take a bath, but fortunately, she did not suffer any embarrassment.

The government responded to the co-operation between government departments and volunteer agencies by establishing new programmes covering assured income, aids for daily living, and new transportation grants.

Later, in 1981, the International Year of Disabled Persons (I.Y.D.P.) proved to be a challenge and an opportunity to make the public more aware of the needs of the handicapped, as well as to determine the future direction of services and agencies.

The objective of the UN draft for a Long-Term World Plan of Action was "to propose concrete measures which could contribute to bringing about a radical change in the situation of disabled persons in all aspects of living."

In 1975, the UN had defined a "disabled person" as: "any person unable to ensure by himself or herself, wholly or partly, the necessities of a normal individual and/or social life as a result of a deficiency, either congenital or not, in his or her physical or mental capabilities."

This was adopted in Canadian legislation.

As part of the provincial package for public awareness, plans were initially made for a workshop during I.Y.D.P. on "Future Direction for Rehabilitation Services in Alberta". This was eventually dropped at the request of the Premier in favour of a

Committee for International Year of the Disabled Person (1981).

This committee, chaired by Judge Brian Stevenson, recommended the establishment of a provincial task force by, and directly responsible to, the Executive Council of the Provincial Government to co-ordinate legislation, policies and programmes pertaining to disabled persons in Alberta; and that the Executive Council appoint a Minister responsible for all areas concerning the needs of disabled persons.

An amusing aside to this committee was the appointment of Judge Brian Stevenson as chairman. I asked the judge how he had been appointed to the committee in view of the fact that he had been the premier's Liberal opponent in the provincial elections. He assured me they were good and respectful friends. In fact, at the last election, Premier Lougheed had telephoned the judge to ascertain if he was going to compete again. In reply, Judge Stevenson reminded him that the last contest had led to a premiership; another encounter might lead to the prime minister's chair, and he wasn't going to take the risk.

At a federal level, Canada in June 1980 hosted the XIVth World Congress of Rehabilitation International in Winnipeg. This major event had several thousand delegates from around the world, and focused on the needs and aspirations of the disabled. It was also the springboard to launch the International Year of Disabled Persons.

In February of 1981 "Obstacles", the Report of the Special Committee on the Disabled and the Handicapped, was published. The Chairman, David Smith, stated that the purpose of the report was to identify the key obstacles faced by disabled persons in Canada, and to outline practical actions which would help to overcome these obstacles. Disabled persons were not asking for a "hand-out" but for a "hand-up" so that they could build for themselves lives of independent choice and action.

This was followed by the report of the Canadian organizing committee for 1981, entitled "Directions". I was fortunate to serve on this committee and on the parallel provincial committee.

The report "Directions" was published "to share the experience of the International Year of Disabled Persons" with as many people as possible, as well as to provide some directions for those whose work continued beyond 1981. It contained descriptions of some programmes and highlights which occurred during the year. It also featured 65 recommendations for action in several crucial subject areas such as architectural accessibility, education, employment, independent living, prevention and transportation.

Thus the year 1981 ended with optimism and hope for the future. In the words of the Co-Chairperson, Yvonne Raymond, in the report "Directions", it "was the year when the seeds of hope and dreams were sown... these seeds will sprout and society will reap the harvest in years to come."

Just prior to the I.Y.D.P., the Calgary community submitted their plan to government for approval. Its title was "Feasibility Study, Resources for Handicapped People – A Calgary Community Plan 1978". This plan called for the redeployment of the resources from the Baker Centre, as well as other new services for the developmentally handicapped.

The timing of the report was fortuitous because shortly after we had received the report we were informed by the Public Works Division that the buildings were in need of major repairs and that their life span was now very limited.

We had already demonstrated the ability of community residences to meet the needs of many of these severely handicapped children. The plan therefore called for a programme of regulated closure of villas with the transfer of residents to community facilities in the region. Of the 200 residents, only 60 were considered in need of very specialised facilities. It was therefore recommended that small clusters of group homes with connecting specialised support systems be strategically placed throughout the city for the latter group.

However, the political climate had changed. The emphasis was on spreading more resources into the rural areas, and because of a downturn in the economy, a much closer examination of operational costs. Some of these costs would be off-set by the transfer of staff and operational costs from the Baker Centre; but after a number of projections and review, the cost of a 60-bed unit still proved to be less than our preferred options.

The minister therefore decided that a 60-bed unit should be built in a rural area, and that it be attached to a local hospital. I was very concerned about this on two accounts:

1. It could be a return to institutional care and contrary to the ideals and hopes expressed in the Calgary community plan.
2. There was the real possibility of losing the supportive relationship we had with the paediatric specialists – and could a rural district provide the required professional staff and expertise?

In response to my protests, the minister arranged for me to meet the rural members of the legislature, and after a rather passionate discussion the rural representatives held to their position, but they did agree that there should be two facilities of 30 beds each. It was agreed that one should be in Bow Island – a community with a population of about 2000, and Fort McLeod with a population of just over 3000, which was in the Lethbridge Com-Serv region.

Following this, a number of meetings were held with the hospital boards and medical and nursing staff, and the university paediatric unit agreed to provide training and back-up arrangements. We worked very closely with the hospital boards and staff in the design of the new facilities, and ensured that the design would allow for the facilities to be used in the future for long-term or geriatric care if and when they were not required by the severely or profoundly handicapped individuals. These individuals were all regarded as medically dependent or medically at risk.

The plan envisaged five individual apartments under one roof with a central core area and a corridor connecting to the hospital. Each apartment was to have three bedrooms, kitchenette, living-room and two bathrooms. In the central core there were offices, overnight visitors' rooms, two personal-care rooms, a doctor's examination room, nurses' station, physio and occupational therapy workshop, conference room, and a large activity room which had a gymnasium and three classrooms.

The Bow Island facility was the first to be opened. It was known as the Alfred Egan Home, and was built at a cost of 4.5 million dollars in May 1985; the other opened in September 1985.

Unfortunately by the time the facilities were built I had left the department. With the downturn in the economy and reduced pressure on government as the result of the rapid growth in community services for the handicapped, the government adopted the age-old solution, reorganization. In spite of the fact that we had experienced teams in central and regional offices who had been together for almost ten years and had established strong links with the community, the government decided to "streamline" the services by dispensing with the Division of Services for the Handicapped and dispersing staff to the regional social services administration. I was to become a consultant to the services, but the terms of reference for such a position were not clear, and the loss of our multi-disciplinary team confirmed my decision. It was time for a change and a new challenge.

CHAPTER 15

FULL CIRCLE

It was 1953 when I received my diploma in Public Health and I embarked on a new career. My plan was to become involved in industrial medicine in the hope of preventing the chronic and tragic cases I had seen when practising medicine in mining and agriculture communities.

Somehow, my new ambition was side-tracked and for almost thirty years I was occupied with the problems associated with chronic disabling handicaps, with few of these being the result of industrial accidents, and with public health.

Now in May 1982 I became involved, not in the prevention of industrial accidents, but in the assessment and rehabilitation of these workers. I started as a medical officer with the Alberta Workers' Compensation Board.

This change was quite a challenge as I was forced to refresh and upgrade my knowledge of clinical medicine, orthopaedics and post-traumatic conditions. It was many years since I had examined for low-back injuries and such conditions as injuries to knees, wrists and shoulders. Fortunately, I received considerable help from my medical colleagues.

With a general practitioner, Dr. Earl Ghitter, we entered the realm of the board, and for a week or so we felt we had obtained a very pleasant sinecure. We leisurely learned the workings of the board and, between cups of coffee, looked at some files.

However, this soon changed when we were attached to a unit in head office to review files in order to ensure that all medical investigations had been completed, and to check and review reports and clarify any discrepancies.

There was a severe backlog in the files to be reviewed, and being accustomed to long and sometimes irregular hours, we frequently continued working beyond normal working hours. This resulted in us being told that we were setting a bad example.

Soon after we were transferred to the rehabilitation centre in Edmonton where we each had our team of physiotherapists, occupational therapist, a psychologist and a case manager.

As a member of the team we would perform a general physical assessment of the worker to ascertain the history and problems, to give him or her appropriate counselling or education regarding the medical or orthopaedic condition, and to liaise or refer for consultation with the outside physician or specialist. X-rays and laboratory investigation were also carried out when required.

Towards the end of the day the team met to compare the results of their respective assessments and to decide on a programme. These meetings were very fruitful, with amazing consistency and agreement in the analysis of the problems and treatment.

An essential part of teamwork in these cases is good record-keeping, and this needs a very competent secretary, not only to type the reports, etc, but also to ensure that each member has copies of the relevant papers.

I was fortunate to have Susan Meeds who was very efficient and equally pleasant and persuasive when dealing with workers, team members, and of course, myself. At times she was supported by Chris Umrysh who would enliven any company. Later when I reached retirement age, they ensured that this event did not go unnoticed.

Examination of workers was always very interesting. Most of the workers were genuine, but of course we had our share of men and women who, to put it mildly, exaggerated their disability.

Partial undressing was not only revealing from a clinical point of view, but it also helped to expose any masquerade. For example, the worker who was so crippled with low-back pain that he could not reach his hands to his knees when asked to bend forward, miraculously could bend forward to untie his shoelaces or pick up his cigarette packet when it fell out of his pocket.

It was also sometimes very illuminating to stand at my office door to watch a suspect approach for his examination, especially if his injury involved his leg. The rehabilitation centre was built around a central court with walls covered with glass so that it was possible to observe anyone walking around the perimeter. It was interesting to see the change in his stride when he reached the home stretch.

Prolonged unemployment due to an injury can be very discouraging, and often leads to feelings of guilt and insecurity. This was exemplified in the following case. This lady had been off work for months and thought she would never be able to return to her job. Her injury, which caused intense pain in her upper right arm, resulted from constantly lifting heavy food boxes and slicing meat during her 15 years of employment with a downtown department store.

This deli manageress saw a number of doctors, but none were able to instil confidence in her, and she remained at home. When she was referred to the centre she was very apprehensive and "she pictured the worst". After three months of daily programmes, including physiotherapy, psychology and relaxation classes, she returned to work doing what her job dictated with slight variations in the amount of heavy lifting. She summed up her experience thus:

> *"Rehabilitation is just like a job – with the effort and*
> *time that's devoted in rehabilitation, you get out of it*
> *what you put in. I figure everything they did for me*
> *at the centre and my positive attitude towards my*
> *rehabilitation helped me recover to my former self."*

Workers also are frequently confused by or misapprehend the cause or the mechanics of their injury – this was particularly so in back injuries. Moreover, the different forms of investigation and treatment also confused the worker. Should I have surgery? What is a bone scan?... and so on.

The centre had a back education programme, but there were a number of criticisms from staff and workers. In typical fashion I soon found myself chairing an inter-departmental committee to study the back education programme and to make recommendations.

As a result, we introduced a new programme which involved all the departments, and I was landed with the medical programme – this included looking at the structure of the back, disabilities, investigations and treatment, with question and answer periods.

Another injury, which fortunately was not as common as back injuries but more perplexing, was brain injury. Perhaps because of my psychiatric background, I joined the team in addition to my regular responsibilities.

Seriously brain-injured workers are usually treated in hospital or as out-patients during the acute or pre-chronic phase. The objective of the rehabilitation programme was to assist these workers in their adjustment to the sequelae of brain injury and help restore them to the degree of well-being necessary to return to a suitable and rewarding employment.

In addition to the needs of the brain-injured workers, the relatives and families frequently needed support and other

social services, which impacted on other government departments. We did not feel it was appropriate for us to parallel the
community services. Thus we approached the Department of
Social Services for help. We met with representatives of the
department and concluded that help was needed at two levels
– one at policy level, as several government departments could
be involved, and at the field level there was a need for closer
contact between the departments. This need for more involvement of Community Services was reviewed by the Rehabilitation Centre Planning Committee, which was established at a
later date.

In the midst of my regular routine in the rehabilitation centre, I received, without any warning or consultation, a letter
from the Alberta College of Physicians and Surgeons notifying
me that the college had submitted my name to the Alberta
Solicitor General as their representative on the Rehabilitation
Practitioner Committee of the Alberta Health Disciplines Board.

Naturally, I felt honoured, and very interested, because of
my previous involvement with the rehabilitation practitioner
training programmes. The Health Disciplines Act was proclaimed in 1981. The purpose of this act was to protect the
public by ensuring that practitioners in health disciplines, which
were previously unregulated, met acceptable standards, and
were registered. The role of the board was to assess the need
for a health discipline to be regulated under the act, and to
advise the minister of its findings. If a discipline is recognised
under the act, the board is then responsible for developing
standards and regulations for the practitioners.

Another committee in which I participated was more mundane; it was the Christmas Concert Committee for 1986. We
decided to resurrect the show in the rehabilitation centre after
a ten-year absence. On December 18th, the day of the perfor-
mance, everything was set – costumes, music, sound, lights,
video camera – everyone was rehearsed but nervous. The Work
Evaluation Team kicked off with "The Twelve Days of Treat-

ment". This was a parody of one man's plight through the rehabilitation centre.

The medical secretaries, dressed as the seven dwarfs, sang the W.C.B. version of "Heigh-Ho, Heigh-Ho", the psychologist's orchestra was not very symphonic, and the physiotherapy "Flappers" danced the Charleston to a wild cheering crowd who insisted on an encore. As for me, I made the mistake of appearing in full highland regalia to play on my piano accordion a selection of Scottish tunes. To give some variety, I interspersed the music with a few Scottish jokes. I was very surprised by the exuberant response to my jokes until I found that each time I told a joke, a physiotherapist appeared on stage, complete with a long stick which had a mirror at one end, and used this to find out what a Scotsman did wear under his kilt.

The director of the centre, Bob Leenders, in his closing remarks suggested that the staff had put themselves up for evaluation and scrutiny, which is often how a worker at the centre might feel. The workers responded by giving us a standing ovation.

More surprises were to follow. I was due to retire in June 1987, but the board asked if I would continue for another year because of a shortage of physicians and also because I was involved in planning some reorganization within the centre. In the end I agreed to stay until March 1988, when we were scheduled to travel with friends for a prolonged vacation.

Hence I was working on my 65th birthday, and as I was driving to the centre, I switched on my car radio to hear the announcement that I had been chosen as C.F.R.N.'s Sweetheart for the day and to wish me a Happy Birthday.

Continuing on my way, I was further embarrassed when signs started to appear by the roadside stating "Happy 65th Birthday Dr. Short"; another one said "You may be getting older, but you'll never grow up", and yet another "Dr. Short: you're not old, just a recycled teenager".

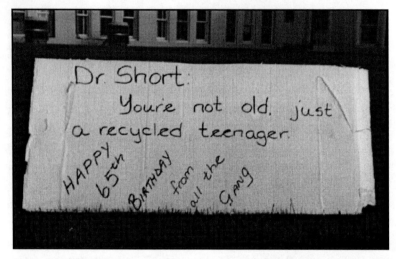

When I arrived at the centre it was to cheers and congratulations from staff and workers, and my office was decorated with balloons and streamers. Later when entering the staff dining-room I was confronted by a birthday cake and a man hired from an entertainment firm to bring me birthday wishes. I had just returned from a vacation in Holland, and the gentleman was dressed as "Zelda" from Amsterdam.

My composure had previously been undermined when we were invited to a friend's birthday party about a week before my birthday. The event was organised by our Scottish country dancing group at our host and hostess's acreage. I was expecting a "roasting", as I had participated in quite a few. A "roasting" in Alberta was when friends surprised the celebrant with songs, poems, anecdotes and amusing gifts which were not too expensive but appropriate for the occasion. This time I reassured myself that our hostess was indeed celebrating her birthday.

We started with a barbecue, and congratulations and best wishes to our hostess. Afterwards we retired into a barn, and then I soon realised that I was the victim. The M.C. announced that one of the gang would recite a poem in celebration of our honoured guest.

The title was "Ode to Richard Short – Dickie the Doc or Short the Shrink". This was followed by more stories and songs, and later, two sketches to remind me of telling too many tales. My "menopausal baby", the one I delivered in Bishop Auckland, was portrayed most effectively, although by the time "the actress" was near full-term her condition was blatantly obvious. The "doctor" was resplendent in white coat and stethoscopes and it took us some time to identify the lady's "mother".

The other sketch demonstrated how I did not carry out the medical assessment of a W.C.B. worker – although the opposite was professed.

One friend, who was in the printing business, had printed a number of cards for me, which gave the telephone numbers of important people, including Ronald Reagan, Mikhail Gorbachev, the Queen, the Pope, Dr. Helmut Kohl, the German Federal Chancellor at that time, and at the end, my name and telephone number with my designation as Pill Pusher.

The party finished with a singsong, which lasted well into the night.

Moving from the ridiculous to the sublime, in 1986 I was appointed to the Rehabilitation Centre Planning Group. The reason for the establishment of this committee was to help in the planning and implementation of a new Service Delivery Model. The planning committee reported to a steering committee in central office, which was headed by the W.C.B. Vice-Chairman.

The purpose of the planning committee, as expressed by the chairman, was to ensure that injured workers, those who may have potential problems of rehabilitation, are identified and dealt with in a timely fashion so that they don't carry on to become chronic.

Studies had shown that the probability of returning to work is reduced to 25 percent after six months, 50 percent after one year and almost nil after two years. A high proportion of the rehabilitation centre admissions were over six months between injury and admission, and the percentage had increased. Costs had more than doubled between 1981 and 1986 for compensation over 45 days, i.e., from $11.5 million to over $24 million. Because of the chronicity of these cases, the average length of stay in the centre tended to be longer.

We therefore put together a model that started with the acceptance of the claim, and how the claim should be handled in central office. We identified criteria, which could be used to identify potential problems, and also identified the case management group which would be responsible for managing the case, either through community resources or at the rehabilitation centre. We also recommended that a pilot project be started as soon as possible.

It should, however, be noted that the need for early intervention was not new. One of the medical officers, Dr. Fowler, writing in the Annual Report 1961 stated, "Experience continues to prove conclusively that disabilities are lessened, time loss reduced, and psychological complications avoided, with earlier referrals and the resulting continuity of treatment". Time will tell if we continue to make the same mistakes.

Returning once more to the more sanguine outlook on life, the final surprise of my professional career occurred with the concert arranged for my retirement. The event was widely advertised throughout the centre, and I was under a lot of pressure to dress in my kilt for the occasion – but I steadfastly refused. The centre closed at mid-day for rehabilitation so that the celebrations could start. You can therefore imagine my surprise when my wife and family arrived with my kilt and other paraphernalia. After I had dressed I was met by a group of our Scottish country dancing friends and was informed that part of the concert programme included my wife and me leading for two demonstration dances.

Members of the board, central office staff, the centre staff, Dr. Graham Clarkson, my Scottish country dancing friends, and my wife, son and his family attended the event.

The M.C. announced that the concert was about "Voices from the Past", and it was then that I was very sorry for relating past experiences to staff in the cafeteria. My past began to be revealed in explicit detail, but some of it was certainly concocted.

I was offered recompense for my bus fare when I had to travel with a nurse – and pay her fare – when we went for our first home delivery – remember we delivered twins.

Then our dining with the Queen Mother was remembered by the palace sending a representative to read a telegram and to wish me a happy retirement. A staff member with a very cultured voice wished me well and then presented me with a cheque for twenty-five pence, stating this was the amount owed by the Royal Family, and would I now please call off the collection agency.

Dr. Graham Clarkson reminded the audience of my foibles in New Brunswick, included my mistake over Dalhousie University.

We then performed our Scottish country dances, only to be flustered when one of the couples in our set became confused during one of the dances and we had great difficulty in extricating ourselves.

A musical choir sang their version of "A Scottish Doctor", and the last chorus introduced the next act. The chorus was:

"Now those cold hands, will no more freeze backs,
Will no more tease backs,
Will no more squeeze backs,
As long as those hands, stay inside his jeans
He won't have to spend a bean."

The examination of a worker with a back injury, as portrayed by staff, could hardly be described as complimentary to my professional expertise.

In fact later in the programme the W.C.B. representative stated that he had always regarded me as a very professional and competent member of the staff until he witnessed this episode.

Of course my visit to Amsterdam was not forgotten. There was a message from "Zelda" who had helped me celebrate my 65th birthday, saying she couldn't attend but sent one of her professional colleagues. Her representative was a member of our female staff who had great difficulty standing upright because of the massive protuberance of her chest, and it created some difficulty when she attempted to kiss me.

Among the presents I received was a lumbar support belt with a tartan lining from Eric Lautischer, our orthotic technician who felt I deserved one considering the number I had prescribed.

The celebration lasted most of the afternoon and was a very happy and memorable occasion for me, which helped to relieve the tension and sadness of saying farewell to so many friends and colleagues.

Within a few days of retirement, we were winging our way with friends for a prolonged vacation to Hawaii, New Zealand and Australia.

CHAPTER 16

POSTSCRIPT

A few months after our very enjoyable vacation we moved to the town of Qualicum Beach on Vancouver Island so that we could get away from the prolonged winters of the Prairies, from frequent snow shovelling and icy winds. It was the end of October 1988 when we moved into our new home. The Island's monsoon period had just started with heavy rain and heavy low clouds which contrasted with the brilliant skies of Alberta, where the clouds always seemed to be at a higher elevation.

To add to our discomfort, our furniture was several days late in arriving, and a number of items were damaged. Our new refrigerator and stove, or cooker, also failed to materialise as planned.

Because of the rain we could not attempt any work outside the home or enjoy leisurely walks. As we were strangers to the town, we had no friends or social activities to help pass the time, which was a marked change from our social life in Edmonton, Alberta.

By mid-December we felt we had made a mistake by moving to the Island, even though we had the Robertson's son Duncan, and his family, to whom we were very attached, living in Victoria. We also had other friends in Victoria, but Victoria was over two hours drive from our home. A number of factors had prevented us from settling in Victoria.

Consequently, we decided to visit our daughter and her family in Kitimat, B.C. which was about 800 miles north of Vancouver. We stayed there until the middle of January.

When we flew back into Vancouver in bright sunshine and saw the green fields and trees, which differed so much from the bleak cold winter of the north, we knew we had made the right decision.

What changes should we make? We decided to join in as many of the local activities as we could, and within a very short time our calendar was full and we were making good friends with retirees who were in the same boat. We were able to relax in warm sunshine, on well-manicured golf courses located in beautiful surroundings, and with the many other pleasures associated with the sea.

I became involved with the town's emergency services for natural disasters, and served as Co-ordinator of Emergency Health and Social Services until the fall of 1994. At this time I was appointed by the provincial government to the Mount Arrowsmith Community Health Council. Our primary responsibility was in the planning and co-ordination of health services, and identifying local health priorities.

We set up a Technical Advisory Group Structure with representation and input from the professions and a Community Co-ordinating Committee comprising voluntary agencies and citizens from the local community. We produced our first draft of our "Health and Management Plan" in January 1996.

There was a great deal of enthusiasm for the government's "New Directions", which resulted from a 1991 Royal Commission on Health Care and Costs; the Commission called for decentralisation, and 21 regional health boards and 80 community health councils were established around the province of British Columbia.

Our enthusiasm as voluntary representatives was soon curbed when, towards the end of 1996, the provincial government announced the demise of community health councils; regional health boards were to continue.

Meanwhile in Alberta there were interesting developments. In a "News Release" dated October 22nd, 1997, the provincial government announced the appointment of a Persons with Developmental Disabilities (P.D.D.) Board, a Foundation Board responsible for fundraising and managing endowments for capital purchases, research and pilot projects, and in addition, six community boards.

This was followed in April 1998 by the signing of an agreement, which allowed regional boards to assume responsibility for delivery of services in the community.

In the words of the Minister of Family and Social Services:

> *"This is the final step in transferring delivery responsibility for services for persons with developmental disabilities to community management. This new community-based structure will give local communities more opportunities to plan and deliver services that specifically meet the unique needs of adults with developmental disabilities in their region."*

Developmental and acquired disabilities can be a scourge to many people, and to a few it can probably be regarded as a blessing. In the latter case, I think of our blind physiotherapist in the hospital in Dovenby who inspired many by his gifts.

Nevertheless, "Those who are maimed or marred... would consider it wonderful to be whole and straight." Let's pray that the efforts of scientists in the field of biotechnology will help to reduce or remove some of the obstacles that prevent anyone from living a full life. Other solutions are in our own hands: the legacy of infants damaged by the excessive consumption of alcohol and drugs by mothers during pregnancy is revolting, and the emotional stresses induced to-day by the pressures from our society can add to the problem.

It is also apparent that our current desire to be politically correct can produce obstacles to the availability of support and information. For example, it required considerable effort on my part to find the names and addresses of the provincial and national voluntary associations for the mentally handicapped. The national association is now called the Canadian Association for Community Living. If this search proved to be a frustration to me, could it not be a serious and confusing dilemma to parents of handicapped children?

Finally I would like to quote from a speech by a 16-year-old girl with cerebral palsy. She won the gold medal for public speaking at the National Wheelchair Games in Montreal 1975:

> *"To fulfil dreams, the individual must have persistence, man must summon strengths to conquer disappointments and defeat, and bear them with dignity, without self-pity; for it is determination, not tears, that makes pain bearable. Sometimes a task when viewed from a distance seems insurmountable, but with a clear mind and patience enough to go on, one step after another, the job gets done. It is said, it is not the mountain that defeats us but the pebbles along the way."*

RICHARD SHORT

The author was born in 1922 and graduated in 1946. He is married with a son and daughter. Hobbies include music, golf, badminton and Scottish country dancing. His professional career encompassed general medical practice, public health, and the administration of community services for the mentally ill, and the mentally and physically handicapped.

EXCERPT FROM THE 1969 ANNUAL REPORT OF THE HEALTH DEPARTMENT OF THE CITY OF EDINBURGH

"A major tragedy of the inclusion of community mental health in the new Social Work Department was the loss to Edinburgh by emigration of Dr. Richard Short who had not only been the architect of the merger of our mental health service with hospital psychiatry but he was also responsible for major advances in the co-ordination of services for the disabled which are unique in Britain. He was untiring in his efforts to help people in need, and contributed so much more to rehabilitation of the handicapped and mentally ill than will ever be achieved by the misguided enthusiasts who contrived to add mental health to their social work empire. He takes with him to his new post in Fredericton, New Brunswick, our warmest wishes for happiness and even greater success than he achieved in Edinburgh."

ISBN 155212452-5

9 781552 124529